KOKO'S GUIDE TO AUSTIN

JANE KO

A TASTE OF KOKO

Dedicated to the city of Austin —
the local businesses, restaurants, and people
who make it the greatest city in the world.

TABLE OF CONTENTS

PRICING KEY

$ under $10 $$$ $31-$60
$$ $11-$30 $$$$ above $61

DEAR AUSTIN,

I moved to Austin, Texas in 2007 to go to school at The University of Texas at Austin (Hook 'em, Horns!) and little did I know that I would fall in love with this town and become a permanent resident.

While I was a student, I—like many of my peers—began thinking about what my career would look like after graduation. The year was 2010, and there were only a few blogs on the internet, but I was immediately drawn to this new form of media. I thought these bloggers were so courageous and it inspired me to start one of my own. *A Taste of Koko* was originally a place for me to publish recipes, and although I didn't have any readers (and Instagram didn't exist), I continued to put out content. It wasn't until after I published my first restaurant review that it began garnering some traffic, which led to the eventual pivot of my blog focus to reflect that.

It's crazy to think about how far *A Taste of Koko* has come since then. I've had the privilege of documenting and sharing eight years of my restaurant experiences. Some standout memories for me include meeting Eric Silverstein of The Peached Tortilla when he parked his food truck outside of my college apartment for his very first day of service, meeting Jae Kim of Chi'Lantro BBQ when he had only one food truck, sharing kimchi fries with Chef Aarón Sánchez on camera for *Food Network*, and being gifted an Uchi cookbook signed by Chef Tyson Cole and Chef Philip Speer.

The city itself has also evolved in so many ways. At some point, Austin became a hot, desirable destination, not only for visitors, but for people looking to settle down somewhere new. And, even though the traffic here sucks, this level of growth has made way for new, innovative restaurants and creative businesses.

This book has truly been a labor of love. Over the course of eight years, I've eaten at hundreds of restaurants, photographed millions of images, and responded to hundreds of inquiries about where to eat and what to do in Austin. I poured my heart out onto these pages—honoring the food, the people, and the energy of the city. I don't know if I can ever fully express my gratitude for how amazing Austin is and how much I love this city, but I hope that this book speaks to that feeling.

Whether you live here or are visiting, I urge you to explore, eat, and enjoy all that Austin has to offer.

Koko

BEST OF:
BREAKFAST

PHOEBE'S DINER

BIRD BIRD BISCUIT

east • $

The early bird gets the freshly baked biscuit sandwiches and dough-doughs (biscuit doughnut holes).

CAFÉ NO SÉ

south congress • $$

Sunny cafe inside South Congress Hotel that serves a delicious, healthy-ish breakfast.

CENOTE

central + east • $

Cozy coffee shop that offers breakfast with organic eggs, local and organic produce, and gluten-free pastries.

CISCO'S RESTAURANT

east • $

A simple menu with food done well. This diner is so legendary, the City of Austin recognized it as a historic landmark.

ÉPICERIE

central · **$$**

Intimate cafe servin French-American comfort food with hot beignets all day.

JOE'S BAKERY

east · **$**

Cooking simple but satisfying breakfast—like the huevos ranchero plate—to happy customers for decades! Pick out a pan dulce while you wait for your table.

JUAN IN A MILLION

east · **$**

Despite countless appearances on *Food Network*, this gem keeps an unassuming vibe, affordable prices, and bountiful servings. I dare you to take on The Don Juan Taco Challenge.

JUNE'S ALL DAY

south congress · **$$**

Chic cafe on SoCo inspired by Spanish tapas bars, Parisian cafes, and hipster NYC wine bars.

KERBEY LANE CAFE

north + south + east + west + central • $

Known for its pancakes and queso, the family-owned Kerbey Lane diners are a solid pick for starting the day or winding down a late night.

MAGNOLIA CAFE

south congress + south • $

Quirky decor and familiar food, this 24-hour diner still embodies the old Austin vibe that they started with in 1988.

PAPERBOY

east + south lamar • $

Stop by this cute pink trailer for the local paper, coffee, and breakfast sandwiches made with locally sourced ingredients.

PHOEBE'S DINER

south 1st • $

Classic American diner with a Texas BBQ flair in South Austin.

PICNIK

central + south lamar • $

Gluten-free restaurant (brick & mortar at central location) with vegan, keto, and paleo options. Fill up on one of their signature butter coffees or the Harvest Hash.

ROCKSTAR BAGELS

east • $

OG bagel shop in Austin pays homage to the traditional New York-style bagel, freshly baked seven days a week.

TACODELI

north + central + downtown + south + west • $

Austin's favorite breakfast tacos made with local and organic ingredients. Be sure to try their Salsa Doña® (if you think you can handle the heat).

VERACRUZ ALL NATURAL

north + south + east • $

Hands down, these are my favorite breakfast tacos in Austin. The migas taco is my go-to and has been rated #4 Best Taco in the US by *Food Network*!

BEST OF:
LUNCH

EL CHILITO

AUSTIN DAILY PRESS

east • $

Tortas (loaded hot sandwiches), tacos , snacks and salads that are perfect for a quick, grab & go lunch.

BLUE DAHLIA

east + west • $$

European-inspired cafe with soups, salads, and sandwiches. Best known for their tartines.

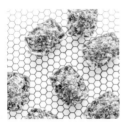

CHI'LANTRO BBQ

north + central + downtown + south lamar • $

Mexican staples meet Korean BBQ flavors at Chi'Lantro—rice bowls, burgers, tacos, and the original kimchi fries.

EL CHILITO

east + south • $

Extensive taco list to choose from but I recommend getting the puffy tacos (or turning any of their regular tacos into a puffy taco).

ELIZABETH ST. CAFE

south 1st • **$$**

A super cute cafe serving up French-Vietnamese fusion. This eclectic menu includes spring rolls, bánh mì, pho, bún, escargot, and pastries.

FAREGROUND

downtown • **$**

With six restaurants and a bar inside and outside, Austin's first food hall has something for everyone.

FOODHEADS

central • **$**

Made-to-order sandwiches and soups in a cozy home that's BYOB and BYOW.

HILLSIDE FARMACY

east • **$**

One of my favorite spots for lunch—I like the Farmacy plate and kale Caesar salad with a side of malt vinegar fries.

HOME SLICE PIZZA

central + south congress • **$**

Pepperoni & margherita pizza is my go-to but try to ask for the off-menu Sicilian-style square pizza if it's not sold out.

HOPDODDY

north + central + south congress • **$**

Don't be intimidated by the wraparound line at Hopdoddy—it moves quickly, and the burgers are so worth it. I had my first burgasm here in 2010.

JOSEPHINE HOUSE

central • **$$**

Feeling fancy? Join the ladies who lunch at this Clarksville cottage. My favorites for lunch are the seasonal rice bowl or big chopped salad.

LA BARBECUE

east • **$$**

Brisket, beef ribs, sausage, and all the sides—if you're not in a meat coma by the end of your meal, you didn't do it right.

P. TERRY'S

north + south + east + west + downtown ● $

Austin's version of fast-food: all-natural, never frozen ingredients. Their beef and chicken options are great, but the veggie burger is a real standout.

SECOND BAR + KITCHEN

north + downtown ● $$

Enjoy a midday meal with a view of the city at either the downtown or Domain NORTHSIDE location.

SOUR DUCK MARKET

east ● $

Casual, all-day bakery and counter service restaurant for a quick bite when you're on the go.

TORCHY'S

north + south + east + west + downtown + s. 1st + s. congress ● $

Everyone needs to eat at Torchy's at least once in their life. No matter what kind of taco you get, your meal isn't complete unless you have their iconic chips and queso.

BEST OF:
DINNER

40 NORTH

downtown • $$

Neapolitan-style pizza, small plates, beers, and a curated wine list in a cozy bungalow.

KOKO TIP: Order the hot honey pizza.

ATX COCINA

downtown • $$

Love this modern Mexican restaurant for their masa-forward offerings. The protein dishes are solid and taste even better paired with a mezcal cocktail.

BUFALINA

east • $$

This Neapolitan pizza spot is a popular option for dinner.

KOKO TIP: If there's a line, put your name down and grab a drink at Eastside Tavern while you wait.

DAI DUE

east • $$

Everything at this local butcher shop comes from local Texas farms. Choose from the a la carte selection or the Supper Club menu.

FRESA'S

south 1st • $$

When people ask me what my favorite restaurants are, Fresa's consistently makes it into my top picks. I always order the queso, chimichurri steak tacos, and a frozen prickly pear margarita.

G'RAJ MAHAL

rainey • $$

My favorite spot for Indian food—start with the batura or garlic naan and order the tikka masala.

KOKO TIP: Don't miss the Indian spice beignets for dessert.

IL BRUTTO

east • $$

Find all of your favorite carbs—from pizza to pasta—at this buzzy Italian spot. (And their frozen Aperol Spritz pairs well with all of it.)

LA CONDESA

downtown • $$

One of my favorite restaurants in Austin for its modern Mexican cuisine and outdoor people-watching patio.

LAUNDERETTE

east ● **$$$**

This former laundromat got the ultimate glow-up. A James Beard finalist restaurant like this one does not disappoint when it comes to new gourmet American fare.

LORO

south lamar ● **$$**

It's no surprise that the love child of Chef Tyson Cole (Uchi/Uchiko) and Chef Aaron Franklin (Franklin Barbecue) resulted in this Asian smokehouse - Texas BBQ fusion.

ODD DUCK

south lamar ● **$$**

James Beard Award nominee Chef Bryce Gilmore wows with a constantly changing small-plates menu focused on sustainable and locally sourced ingredients.

RAMEN TATSU-YA

north + east + south lamar ● **$$**

Ramen Tatsu-Ya opened their first shop in Austin in 2012 and showed us that ramen is so much more than just a tenȼ package with their steaming bowls of tonkotsu broth. Slurrrp!

THE PEACHED TORTILLA

central • $$

Elevated Asian comfort food in dishes like the pork belly bowl, dan dan noodles, Hainan chicken, and tacos.

TITAYA'S

central • $

Familiar Thai dishes with an upscale twist. Confession: I order takeout from Titaya's more times than I'd like to admit.

VIA 313

east + west + central • $$

Detroit-style pizza for anyone who prefers their pizza with an abundance of cheese and sauce on a thick, oh-so-good crust.

YUYO

east • $

Trust me when I say that this food tastes exactly like the upscale cuisine you'd find in Peru. Don't miss the Pisco Sour cocktail!

**BEST OF:
BRUNCH**

SUERTE

BANGER'S

rainey • $$

One word: manmosa. A full bottle of champagne added to orange juice and served in a giant beer-stein glass.

CONTIGO

central • $$

When I want to meet up with a group of my friends, we go to Contigo's farm-to-table Sunday brunch on their spacious patio from 10am–2pm.

EL NARANJO

south lamar • $$

El Naranjo will transport you to Central Mexico with their refined Oaxacan dishes.

FONDA SAN MIGUEL

central • $$$

Fanciest all-you-can-eat brunch buffet in Austin goes to Fonda San Miguel's Sunday. It's around $40, which can be pricey but I promise you get what you pay for.

FRANKLIN BARBECUE

east • **$$**

If you're going to dedicate two to three hours to stand in line at Franklin, the weekend would be your best option.

KOKO TIP: Eat before you go or bring snacks.

JACK ALLEN'S KITCHEN

north + west + south • **$$**

Stuff yourself with chicken fried chicken, migas, and layered enchilada casserole at Jack Allen's all-you-can-eat Sunday brunch for $18.

LA BARBECUE

east • **$$**

There's often a line running out of La Barbecue, but their brisket and beef ribs are so worth it.

KOKO TIP: Buy a beer from the grocery store inside and sip while you wait.

LIN ASIAN BAR + DIM SUM

downtown • **$**

Dim sum for brunch? Lin Asian Bar has soup dumplings, potstickers, sui mai, and more.

MATTIE'S

south congress · $$

Go to Mattie's and dine on the 19th-century home patio for prime viewing of their resident peacocks.

MOONSHINE GRILL

downtown · $$

Moonshine Grill has a popular brunch that's worth waking up early for. For only $18, you can get all the chicken & waffles, grits, ribs, and comfort food you can dream of.

SUERTE

east · $$

One of my favorite newer brunch spots in Austin is Suerte in East Austin for its tacos, tostadas, and homemade Mexican pastries.

TAKOBA

downtown · $$

If you want cheap mimosas with an elevated Mexican brunch, Takoba has $1 mimosas by the glass and $5 carafes.

BEST OF:
DESSERT

AMY'S ICE CREAM

central + east + south congress • $

Austin's original ice cream shop—pick your favorite ice cream, mix-ins, and crush'ns. If you guess their movie quote of the day correctly, they'll give you a free mix-in!

BANANARCHY

central + south 1st • $

Chocolate-dipped frozen bananas with various toppings —need I say more?

CASEY'S NEW ORLEANS

central • $

Fluffy, melt-in-your-mouth snow-balls made with 100% natural juice since 1996.

KOKO TIP: My favorite is the blue coconut with cream.

CHURROS CO.

south 1st + central • $

Perfectly fried churros tossed in cinnamon sugar and topped with scoops of ice cream and sauces.

COW TIPPING CREAMERY

south • $

Think, artisanal soft-serve.
Now, think artisanal soft-serve
with the most ridiculously
creative combination of add-ins.

DOLCE NEVE

south 1st • $

All-natural gelato shop with a
large rotating menu and gelato
pops dipped in chocolate.

FROZEN ROLLS CREAMERY

downtown • $

Thai-style rolled ice cream shop
on North Lamar with fun flavors
and toppings. Half the fun is
watching them make it.

GELATERIA GEMELLI

east • $

Organic and seasonal gelato
handmade in small batches.

KOKO TIP: Earl Grey and
Vietnamese coffee are my
favorites. They have cocktails too.

LICK HONEST ICE CREAMS

central + south lamar • $

Local Austin ice cream shop scooping seasonal artisanal ice cream with local and natural ingredients. Give their quirky flavors a shot—the roasted beets & goat cheese are quite popular.

NADAMOO! SCOOP SHOP

south lamar • $

What started as a vegan ice cream brand at grocery stores recently opened up its own ice cream shop "IRL" in Austin.

PROHIBITION CREAMERY

east • $

Three words: boozy ice cream. Try the deconstructed old-fashioned sundae with bourbon ice cream.

SPUN ICE CREAM

east • $

Watch your ice cream being made before your very eyes with the magic of liquid nitrogen.

RKSIDE

CLARK'S OYSTER BAR

BEST OF: HAPPY HOUR

ODD DUCK

UCHI

ATX COCINA
downtown

Every day, 4:30-6:30pm

$3 off cocktails, wine and draft beer, $4 off select menu items (only at bar/lounge/patio)

BARCHI SUSHI
downtown

Every day, 3-5pm
$4.50 sushi rolls, $5 cocktails

**Reverse happy hour —
Thursday, 10-12am**

Friday & Saturday, 10-12:30am

CLARK'S OYSTER BAR
downtown

Monday to Friday, 3-6pm

Half off burgers, 50¢ off oysters, $5 martinis, oyster shooters, and draft beer

Saturday & Sunday, 3pm-6pm

50¢ off oysters, half off bottles of wine, and $5 oyster shooters

KOKO TIP: Clark's is one of my favorite happy hours because the pan roasted Black Angus Burger is 1/2 off. It's the best burger in Austin and it comes with a mountain of shoestring fries.

GRIZZELDA'S
east

Tuesday to Friday, 5-7pm

$7 house margaritas and draft cocktails, $3, $5, and $8 bites

HILLSIDE FARMACY
east

Monday to Friday, 3-6pm

Half price snacks, $2 off cocktails, beer, and wine

Monday Nights Only:

$5 bubbles & half off oysters

Tuesday Nights Only:

Burger, fries, & old fashioneds for $15

JEFFREY'S
central

**All night Mondays
Tuesday to Sunday, 4:30-6:30pm**

Half price bar food and $2 off each cocktail, beer, and glass of wine

KOMÉ
central

Monday to Thursday, 5-6pm

Discounted appetizers, sushi rolls, and drink specials

LENOIR
south 1st

Tuesday to Sunday, 5-6:30pm

$3 draft beers and $5 wine specials by the glass in the outdoor wine garden

LORO
south lamar

Weekdays, 2-5pm

Exclusive menu items like the Loro burger all under $10, $4 boozy slushees, & 1/2 off select beer, wine, and sake on tap

LUCKY ROBOT
south congress

Monday to Friday, 4:30-6pm

Half price appetizers and select bottles of sake & wine, and $5 & under Lucky Bites

Weekend brunch on Saturday & Sunday, 10:30-11:30am

30% off all brunch dishes

ODD DUCK
south lamar

Sunday to Thursday, 2:30-6:30pm

Drink specials

Sunday to Thursday, 5-6:30pm

Half off food specials

PARKSIDE
downtown

Every day, 5-6pm

Half off the full menu, beer, cocktails, wine, and bubbles by the glass

RED ASH
downtown

Every day, 4:30-6:30pm

Discounted appetizers, salads, small pastas, and $2 off all cocktails, beer, and wines by the glass

SALTY SOW
east

Every day, 4:30-6:30pm

$2 off select cocktails and discounted bites every day from 4:30pm to 6:30pm.

UCHI
south lamar

Every day, 5-6:30pm

$3 - $7 drinks, and $3 - $10 bites

UCHIKO
central

Every day, 5-6:30pm

$3 - $7 drinks, and $3 - $10 bites

BEST OF:
DATE NIGHT

VIXEN'S WEDDING

BAR PEACHED

downtown • $$

Post-dinner-date nightcap from Bar Peached on their large outdoor patio is a wonderful way to wind down the evening.

BARLEY SWINE

central • $$

Shareable small plates that will make any first date become a second date.

CLARK'S OYSTER BAR

downtown • $$

Preppy seafood restaurant with excellent oysters, burger & shoestring fries, and cocktails.

DIPDIPDIP TATSU-YA

central • $$$

Things will get steamy at this new intimate shabu-shabu spot, where hot pot meets steakhouse.

EDEN EAST

east · $$

Dine under the stars and twinkling lights on the Eden East farm with—you guessed it —farm-to-table cuisine.

INTERO

east · $$

Nothing is more romantic than housemade pasta and Italian food. Save room for their handcrafted chocolates!

KEMURI TATSU-YA

east · $$

See how adventurous your date is by ordering one of their funky dishes at this Japanese-Texas fusion izakaya.

KOKO TIP: The Matcha Painkiller in a cat cup is insta-worthy.

OLIVE & JUNE

central · $$

This restaurant just begs for a "Lady and the Tramp" moment with their pasta dishes and stellar wine list. Did I mention it feels like you're dining in a treehouse?

OSEYO

east • $$

Traditional Korean cooking with banchan (small side dishes) in a fine dining restaurant experience.

PITCHFORK PRETTY

east • $$

Proudly serving the soulful tastes of the Hill Country, Pitchfork Pretty's wraparound, covered veranda is a cozy and inviting date-night location.

THE BACKSPACE

downtown • $$

Quaint and cool brick-oven pizza joint that makes the best Neapolitan pizzas and has an extensive collection of Italian wines.

VIXEN'S WEDDING

east • $$$

Boho decor and Goan-Portuguese fusion cuisine. Let loose, eat with your hands, and if the night goes well, you can get a room upstairs.

EBERLY

UCHI

BEST OF:
SPECIAL
OCCASIONS

EMMER & RYE

JUSTINE'S BRASSERIE

ARLO GREY
downtown • $$$

French and Italian inspired menu by Top Chef 10 winner Kristen Kish with a breath-taking view of Lady Bird Lake while you eat.

EBERLY
south lamar • $$$$

Eberly is all glitz and glamour. If you're wanting to impress, take your guests to this stunning space and dine among the Austin elite.

EMMER & RYE
rainey • $$

Emmer & Rye offers an 11-course shared family-style set menu for special occasions. You'll receive a printed personalized menu when you sit down.

JEFFREY'S
central • $$$$

The city's original fine dining restaurant is still the swankiest option for birthdays, anniversaries, and everything in between.

JUNIPER
east • $$

This upscale Italian restaurant does a monthly tasting menu that does not disappoint or leave you hungry.

JUSTINE'S BRASSERIE
east • $$

Love this French restaurant for its romantic patio garden, twinkling lights, and French food and wine. There's a gazebo in the backyard if you want to pop the question.

LAUNDERETTE
east • $$

Swoon over Launderette's snacky bits, wood-grilled entrees, and craft cocktails in a sleek space. Order the birthday cake ice cream sandwich whether it's your special day or not.

LE POLITIQUE
south 1st • $$$

Chic brasserie in downtown with French favorites like steak tartare, escargots, and a variety of frites plates.

LENOIR
south 1st · $$$

Romantic vintage-style setting with a four-course, pre-fixed option for dinner completed with wine pairings. Saunter on over to the wine garden afterwards for a relaxing end to your meal.

OLAMAIE
central · $$$

Here in Texas we're known for our Southern hospitality and the best place for it is at Olamaie.

KOKO TIP: Ask for the off-menu biscuits.

OTOKO
south congress · $$$$

Intimate 12-seat Japanese restaurant doing traditional sushi omakase-style dinner for $215 per person. Tickets are released a season in advance —reservations required.

PERLA'S
south congress · $$$

Whether you enjoy your meal on the airy patio or settle into the spacious dining room, Perla's seafood is exceptional.

SWAY
north + south 1st + west · $$

Upscale Thai restaurant serving spicy dishes will light up your relationship and the community seating will have you making new friends.

UCHI
south lamar · $$$$

Uchi's ten-course chef's tasting omakase is the top choice for special occasions, for both visitors and residents.

UCHIKO
central · $$$$

My top suggestion for date night is always Uchiko. Aside from its elevated sushi experience, many of their dishes, like the Hot Rock Wagyu, come with an experiential element.

UROKO
east · $$$

A 45-minute omakase that only seats four people is hands down the most intimate date night dining experience in Austin. Very exclusive, so plan to make a reservation a month in advance.

MORE HOME SLICE PIZZA

IRENE'S

**BEST OF:
LATE NIGHT**

888 PAN ASIAN

GOURDOUGH'S

24 DINER
downtown • $$

Your classic diner food with a fancy twist in a 24-hour joint. Order one of their signature hashes or go for the chicken & waffles if you're in the mood for a classic. Always wash it down with a milkshake.

888 PAN ASIAN
south • $

Authentic Asian food with a very extensive selection. Get your fix of Thai, Chinese, or Vietnamese food until 2am on most nights. Great for takeout!

BENNU COFFEE
east + south congress • $

I spent too many of my college all-nighters at Bennu Coffee and go there when I need to get work done at odd hours. Plus, they specialize in gourmet mocha drinks.

CASINO EL CAMINO
downtown • $

When the munchies kick in after a night drinking on 6th Street, make your way to Casino El Camino for a big, juicy burger. Get there before they close at 2am.

EASY TIGER
central + downtown • $

Soft pretzels, beer cheese, sausages, and more than 30 local draft beers on tap taste better in the ambience of Easy Tiger's massive beer garden.

EL TAQUITO
south • $

Street tacos available to the inebriated folks until 4am on Friday and Saturday.

GOURDOUGH'S
south 1st + south lamar • $

If your late-night cravings are on the sugary side, get one of their big, fat donuts with gourmet toppings. Not guaranteed to cure a hangover but will definitely hit the sweet spot.

KOKO TIP: My favorite is the Miss Shortcake or Mother Clucker.

IRENE'S
downtown • $

The weekend West 6th Street crowd often finds its way to Irene's for snacks, toasts, and vanilla soft serve.

JAVELINA
rainey • $

You're going to be hungry after a night of drinking on Rainey St. Go to Javelina for Texas burgers, tacos, and even salads until 1:30am.

JUSTINE'S BRASSERIE
east • $$

A romantic, divey, and a little bit hipster atmosphere that does justice to French cuisine.

KERBEY LANE CAFE
north + central + west + south • $

Beloved college student hangout diner for breakfast that's served 24/7.

LA MEXICANA
south 1st • $

Freshly baked Mexican pastries and possibly the most affordable tacos in town available at any hour.

LITTLE DARLIN'
south • $

If you find yourself in South Austin and need a late-night meal, Little Darlin' is open until 2am every night.

MAGNOLIA CAFE
south congress + south • $

With several 24-hour diners in Austin, you'd think the city doesn't sleep, but we just love our breakfast food so much we want it available around the clock.

MORE HOME SLICE
south congress • $

Walk up to More Home Slice for a quick piece of pizza on South Congress until midnight on Friday and Saturday.

MRS. JOHNSON'S
central • $

This bakery is open all night long and has a drive-thru window. Try to go when the 'hot' sign is on and you might get a free donut straight out of the fryer.

KOKO TIP: I always get the donut holes.

VIA 313
east + central • $

I don't know about you, but after a night out, I always crave a thick piece of pizza to help soak up the booze.

BEST OF:
GROUP MEALS

FRESA'S

BANGER'S
rainey · $$

Twenty different housemade sausages and 200+ beers on tap with the largest outdoor patio seating on Rainey Street.

CONTIGO
central · $$

Picnic tables for ample seating and sharable charcuterie boards are perfect for group gatherings.

KOKO TIP: Start with crispy green beans, housemade pickles, and a charcuterie board.

EASY TIGER
downtown + central · $

Easy Tiger's easy boards with pretzels, pastrami, sausages, and cheese are made for sharing.

KOKO TIP: Ask for a chocolate cookie to go before you head out.

FAREGROUND
downtown · $$

Meet up at Fareground so everyone can choose from any of the 6 restaurants, 2 bars, and then reconvene to eat outside on the lawn.

FRESA'S
south 1st · $$

Shareable tacos, queso, Brussels sprouts and more on colorful picnic tables. It's also spacious and inviting for kids!

G'RAJ MAHAL
rainey · $$

The seating in the front of G'raj Mahal might look limited but head to the back for spacious seating. Samosas, pakoras, naan, and batura are great for sharing while your group decides what to order.

HULA HUT
central · $$

Hang out with your crew at Hula Hut's back patio that extends above Lake Austin. Go for the Pu Pu platters if you're looking for an option to share.

IRENE'S
downtown · $

Spread out on the big picnic tables at Irene's and hang out while munching on the appetizers that are best shared with friends.

KOKO TIP: The Nutella toast with banana is my favorite.

47

JACOBY'S

east • $$

Jacoby's family-style sides like pimento cheese grits and fried green beans are perfect for sharing.

MATT'S EL RANCHO

south lamar • $$

Matt's El Rancho can fit up to 500, you know, just in case you're planning a really big group meal.

KOKO TIP: The Bob Armstrong dip, nachos, sizzling fajitas with flour tortillas, and margaritas are perfect for sharing.

NEW FORTUNE CHINESE

north • $

Dim sum is the ultimate group meal where you can order a lot of different dumplings, shu mai, green onion pancake, and more to share.

RANCH 616

downtown • $$

Good for groups because you can be as loud as you want on this rowdy patio (it's on West 6th Street, after all).

THE ABGB

south lamar • $$

There's nothing more perfect for big groups than pizza, sandwiches, and craft brews at a brewery.

THE SALT LICK BBQ

north + west • $$

Their famous all-you-can-eat family-style barbecue is only $24.95 per person and it's BYOB.

KOKO TIP: Driftwood location is cash only.

THE BREWER'S TABLE

east • $$

Sharable feasts in ranch, gulf, and garden options come with three sides. Level up your meal with any of their craft cocktails or choose from the extensive craft beer list.

WU CHOW

downtown • $$

Soup dumplings made from scratch, plus seafood, beer, pork, lamb, and vegetable entrees make it easy to try a little bit of everything. Turn the party up with any of their tiki cocktails.

BEST OF:
COFFEE

BENNU COFFEE
east + south congress

24/7 coffee shop that's frequented by college students especially during finals week.

BETTER HALF COFFEE
downtown

You could easily post up here all day. Start with coffee, end with a beer, and make your way through their gourmet food menu in between.

CAFFÉ MEDICI
central + downtown + south lamar + east

Grandfather of coffee shops in Austin with several locations throughout the city. Many former Caffé Medici baristas have gone on to open their own cafes.

CIVIL GOAT
west

Cutest little coffee shop in West Austin and they have a resident pygmy goat named Butters!

KOKO TIP: Good luck getting any work done, Butters is really cute.

COSMIC COFFEE
south congress

Coffee in the morning and craft beer in the evening. There's live music, dogs, kids, food trucks, and even a chicken coop at Cosmic.

KOKO TIP: Live music is every Tuesday and Sunday.

CUVÉE COFFEE
east

Ethically sourced coffee and cold brewery. Cuvée has turned cold brew into something of an art form, infusing nitrogen to create a drink that's smooth and creamy without the cream.

FIGURE 8 COFFEE
east

If you want the vibes to be as good as the coffee, swing by this quaint neighborhood cafe. (As a plant lady, I appreciate all the greenery in here.)

FLAT TRACK COFFEE
east

Coffee and bikes don't seem like the most obvious pairing, but Flat Track did it and made it really cool.

FLEET COFFEE
east

This tiny little coffee shop serves a mean cup of joe and a seasonally changing cortado.

FLITCH COFFEE
east

Coffee is served from a vintage trailer with a dog-friendly space.

KOKO TIP: Grab a coffee & head down the road to Tillery Plant Co. & East Austin Succulents.

GREATER GOODS
east

Beautifully curated coffee shop that makes an excellent matcha. Take your coffee obsession to the next level by signing up for one of their latte art classes.

HALCYON
downtown + central

Halcyon's downtown location is a popular hangout spot and the Mueller location is sunny and colorful.

KOKO TIP: Tabletop s'mores and coffee martinis make for a cute date idea!

HANK'S
central

One of my favorite coffee shops in Austin.

KOKO TIP: The mint cold brew is my go-to during the summer.

HOUNDSTOOTH
north + east + central + downtown

Expertly crafted coffee where the baristas really know their stuff. Craft cocktails at select locations.

JO'S COFFEE
downtown + south congress

Two locations, but the SoCo spot is where you'll find the iconic "I love you so much" mural. Order the iced turbo.

MAÑANA
south congress

Floor-to-ceiling windows make this inviting coffee shop extra sunny.

MERIT COFFEE
central + downtown + s. lamar

This San Antonio-based coffee shop has quickly become a favorite in Austin.

51

PATIKA
downtown + south lamar

Patika originally started as a tiny coffee trailer and grew to be a hot spot on South Lamar with breakfast and lunch.

RADIO
south austin

Popular coffee spot with food trucks parked outside. They turn off the Wi-Fi in the evenings and on weekends to facilitate a more personal connection.

SA-TÉN
central + east

Japanese coffee shop with drinks like the ohayo (brown sugar cappuccino), plus toasts, sandwiches, and bowls.

KOKO TIP: The toasts and Japanese curry plates are really good.

SEVENTH FLAG COFFEE
south lamar

Want to leave your house for coffee but still feel like you're at home? This place has a smooth brew and relaxed living room vibes.

SUMMER MOON
north + south 1st

Widely known for their magical Moon Milk. The recipe is top secret, but whatever they use is totally raising the bar for lattes.

THUNDERBIRD
central + east

When it's cold, I get the honey nut latte, when it's hot, I get the Thai iced coffee.

TOMS ROASTING CO.
south congress

TOMS—yes, the shoe company—opened up a coffee shop where with every TOMS Roasting Co. product you purchase, they'll provide safe water to a community without access.

WRIGHT BROS. BREW & BREW
east

Chill spot to get a cold brew or a cold *brew* (coffee or beer). The industrial patio is nice for hanging out and taking in the sights of the bustling city.

FLAT TRACK COFFEE

HANK'S

SA-TÉN

HALCYON

BEST OF:
BARS

DOWNTOWN

- Azul Rooftop Bar
- Ellis
- HandleBar
- Kung Fu Saloon
- Living Room
- P6
- Péché
- The Roosevelt Room

RAINEY

- Bar Illegal
- Container Bar
- Craft Pride
- Half Step
- Icenhauer's
- Javelina
- Lucille

EAST

- Ah Sing Den
- Domo Alley-Gato
- Kitty Cohen's
- Last Straw
- Luster Pearl East
- Native
- Nickel City
- Stay Gold
- The Liberty
- Whisler's

SECRET

- Firehouse Lounge
- Floppy Disk Repair Co.
- Garage
- Here Nor There
- Midnight Cowboy
- Small Victory
- Watertrade

DANCING

- Barbarella's
- Broken Spoke
- Cheer Up Charlies
- The Volstead Lounge

LGBT-FRIENDLY

- Cheer Up Charlies
- Highland Lounge
- Oil Can Harry's (OCH)
- Rain on 4th

BEST OF:
BREWERIES

AUSTIN BEERWORKS

NORTH

- Austin Beerworks
- Adelbert's Brewery
- Celis Brewery
- Circle Brewing Co.

CENTRAL

- Black Star Co-Op Pub & Brewery
- Draught House Pub & Brewery

EAST

- Austin Eastciders
- Blue Owl Brewing
- Friends and Allies Brewing
- Hi Sign Brewing
- Hops & Grain
- Lazarus Brewing Company
- Live Oak Brewing Company
- The Brewer's Table
- Southern Heights Brewing Co.
- Zilker Brewing Co.

SOUTH

- (512) Brewing Company
- The Austin Beer Garden Brewing Co.
- Independence Brewing Co.
- St. Elmo Brewing Co.
- Uncle Billy's Brewery

WEST

- Family Business Beer Co.
  FUN FACT: This brewery is owned by *Supernatural* co-star, Jensen Ackles!
- Jester King
- Vista Brewing

BEST OF:
WINE BARS

LENOIR

APT 115
east • $

Intimate wine bar in a converted apartment with only 25 seats that serves wine, craft beer, cheese, and charcuterie.

THE AUSTIN WINERY
central • $$

Three half-glass pours for $16 and four half-glass pours for $20. Munch on charcuterie, olives, and nuts while playing board games here.

AVIARY
south lamar • $$

Fancy but unpretentious wine bar in South Austin that also offers Mediterranean farm-to-table snacks.

FABI + ROSI
west • $$

Cute little homey neighbor-hood restaurant with a Euro-centric wine list.

HOUSE WINE
downtown • $

House Wine has over 100 wines by the glass with selections from all around the world. This is Austin, after all, so expect some live music there too.

JUNE'S ALL DAY
south congress • $$

Named after master sommelier, June Rodil, who is one of 26 women in America to carry that credential. How could it not have a fantastic wine menu?

L'ESTELLE HOUSE
rainey • $

Standing out from the rest of the bars on Rainey Street is L'Estelle, a small wine bar with French-inspired comfort food.

LENOIR
south 1st • $$$

Sip on your red, white, or rose in Lenoir's wine garden while snacking on appetizers.

WINEBELLY
south 1st • $$

The internationally curated wine list is so good it made the list of "Top Wine Bars in the US" by *Food and Wine* magazine.

WINK
downtown • $$$

Put your decision-making skills to the test at Wink. They serve 50+ wines by the glass—you name it, they've got it.

**BEST OF:
HEALTHY**

CAFÉ NO SÉ

BENTO PICNIC
east • $

Clean Japanese bento boxes made with non-GMO, hormone- and antibiotic-free ingredients. You can eat inside or outside or take it to go.

BLENDERS & BOWLS
downtown + east • $

The best place for fresh açaí bowls and smoothies. I always get the Paradise Bowl with pitaya because it's as pretty as it is delicious.

CAFÉ NO SÉ
south congress • $$

Bright café inside South Congress Hotel blends clean eating with delicious at brunch. Their dinner menu has salads and bowls that won't leave you feeling weighed down.

CASA DE LUZ
downtown • $

You'll feel zenned out while dining at Casa De Luz's secret garden. The breakfast, lunch, and dinner are vegan, organic, and gluten-free and the short menu changes daily.

HIGH NOTE
downtown • $$

A fresh and healthy concept crafted by Kerbey Lane. Find fare for keto, paleo, vegan, vegetarian, and gluten-free eating preferences, as well as juices with and without booze.

HONEST MARY'S
north • $

Healthy bowls with locally sourced ingredients that don't skimp on flavor.

JOSEPHINE HOUSE
central • $$

The salads served at lunch are about as fresh as the ambience; they're crisp, clean, and look fabulous.

KOKO TIP: I go here for business lunches.

JUICELAND
north + south + east + west + central + downtown • $

Austin's original juice bar with several locations all over town. Pretty much any smoothie, superfood latte, cold-pressed juice, or immune shot is made to order.

HEALTHY

LEAF
downtown · $$

If you're downtown, pop into Leaf for a freshly tossed salad and take it to go in a biodegradable and compostable container.

MALIBU POKÉ
downtown · $$

This poké shop is originally from Dallas but the SoCal-inspired poké bowls truly are the best in Austin IMO.

PICNIK
central + east + south lamar · $

Butter coffee, bone broth, and a 100% gluten-, corn-, peanut-, and soy-free menu. If you're doing Whole30 or AIP, ask for the Special Diet menu!

SOUP PEDDLER
north + central + south 1st + south lamar · $

The signature soups (eight soups are usually in rotation), hot pressed sandwiches, and fresh salads are a fresh takeaway option for when you're in a hurry but don't want to settle for fast food.

THAI FRESH
south congress · $$

Honest, humble (and mostly gluten-free) Thai cooking by a Thailand native with a sweet vegan ice cream shop in the corner.

THE STEEPING ROOM
central · $$

Balanced bowls, light appetizers, tea sandwiches, soups, salads, and steeped tea. Vegan and vegetarian friendly.

VINAIGRETTE
south congress · $$

Generous salads with organic produce from the owner's 10-acre farm in New Mexico. The wine bar is low-key but awesome.

WHOLE FOODS MARKET
north + downtown + south + east · $

I couldn't not include the Austin-born healthy grocery store with several healthy dining options inside. Salad bar, veggie burger bar, taco bar, sushi bar...and the list goes on!

HIGH NOTE

MALIBU POKE

BLENDERS AND BOWLS

THAI FRESH

CURCUMA

MOTHER'S CAFÉ

**BEST OF:
VEGAN &
VEGETARIAN**

THE VEGAN NOM

THE BEER PLANT

ARLO'S
east + downtown • $

One bite of the bac'n cheezeburger and your mind will be blown that it's vegan.

BISTRO VONISH
central • $

Elevated vegan food truck that makes a killer pan-seared mac & cheese.

CAPITAL CITY BAKERY
east • $

You won't believe the cupcakes and cookies are vegan because they're so moist.

CASA DU LUZ
downtown • $

Straightforward, simple, and made with love like your grandma's home cooking, but all vegan/vegetarian.

CURCUMA
east • $

Plant-based food trailer that puts golden mylk on the map in Austin! They also make tasty superfood coffee drinks, tea tonics, and kitchari bowls.

MOTHER'S CAFÉ
central • $$

An Austin staple since 1980, Mother's is a solid pick for healthy vegetarian and vegan food, tucked away in historic Hyde Park.

NADAMOO! SCOOP SHOP
south lamar • $

All of the ice cream is made with a coconut milk base.

SWEET RITUAL
central • $

Colorful ice cream parlor with gluten-free and vegan scoops. Their shakes and sundaes are also over-the-top incredible.

THE BEER PLANT
central • $

Austin's first vegan gastropub with an impressive selection of vegan comfort food like buffalo cauliflower wings, burgers, and chicken & waffles.

THE VEGAN NOM
east • $

Vegan tacos, burritos, and a bomb nut-free, soy-free mac & cheese made with their homemade queso.

BEST OF:
DOG-FRIENDLY

ROSEWOOD

RESTAURANTS

- Banger's
- Batch
- Contigo
- Easy Tiger
- Fresa's
- Hillside Farmacy
- Jo's Coffee
- Loro
- Mozart's Coffee Roasters
- Perla's
- Rosewood
- P. Terry's
- Sour Duck Market
- TLC Austin
- Torchy's Tacos
- Trace

BREWERIES

- 4th Tap Brewing Co-Op
- Blue Owl Brewing Co.
- The ABGB
- Circling Brewing Co.
- Draught House
- Hi Sign Brewing
- Hops & Grains
- Moontower Saloon
- St. Elmo Brewing Co.
- Uncle Billy's
- Yard Bar

COFFEE

- Better Half Coffee
- Cenote
- Flitch Coffee
- Jo's Coffee
- Mozart's Coffee Roasters
- Radio Coffee
- Wright Bros. Brew & Brew

BARS

- Cosmic Coffee + Beer
- Lustre Pearl East
- Moontower Saloon
- Star Bar
- Yard Bar

OFF-LEASH PARKS

- Red Bud Isle
- Turkey Creek Trail
- Auditorium Shores
- Walnut Creek
- Onion Creek

HOTELS

- Four Seasons
- Hotel Van Zandt
- Hotel Ella
- The Driskill
- The LINE Hotel
- Hotel San Jose
- Hotel Saint Cecilia
- W Hotel

EAST SIDE KING

BURRO CHEESE

GRILLED CHEESE

BURF
CHEESE KIT

BEST OF:
FOOD TRAILERS

Little Lucie
Little Lucy's
MINI DONUTS

Patrizi's

LITTLE LUCY'S

PATRIZI'S

AUSTIN RÔTISSERIE
east · $

French-style roasted rôtisserie chicken with local Texas chicken and baguette sandwiches.

BURRO CHEESE
south congress + rainey · $

Ooey gooey, crunchy gourmet grilled cheeses.

DEE DEE
south · $

Authentic Northern Thai comfort food like laab moo, pad kaprow, and mango sticky rice. Emphasis on "authentic"—the food is very spicy!

EAST SIDE KING
east · $

Japanese street-food truck parked in the back of The Liberty bar. Order the Thai chicken karaage and Brussels sprouts salad.

GARBO'S LOBSTER
rainey · $$

Lobster rolls with lobsters straight out of Maine. Pick from Maine style or Connecticut style—you can't go wrong with either.

HOLLA MODE
downtown · $

Thai-style rolled ice cream food truck with vegan options. Stop by on your way into or out of Zilker Park/Barton Springs.

LITTLE LUCY'S
rainey · $$

Hot mini donuts while bar hopping on Rainey Street.

OOGA BOOGA WAFFLES
central · $

Breakfast, savory, or sweet waffles—stuffed.

PATRIZI'S
east · $

Family-owned, old-school Italian doing homemade pasta and wine.

SOURSOP
south · $

Pan-Asian food truck parked at St. Elmo Brewing Co.

VALENTINA'S
south · $

Tex-Mex and barbeque—in the form of tacos.

DISCADA

VERACRUZ ALL NATURAL

BEST OF:
TACOS

TRILL TAQUERIA

VAQUERO TAQUERIA

DISCADA

east • $

Tiny tacos made discada style (cowboy-wok cooking) with big flavor.

EL PRIMO

south 1st • $

Small roadside stand selling breakfast tacos, burritos, and super tortas. Cash only.

EL TACORRIDO

east • $

Drive-thru Mexican taqueria—order the El Equinox (iced horchata with a shot of espresso) with tacos.

JUAN IN A MILLION

east • $

The legendary Don Juan El Taco Grande taco is just $5.95.

ROSARITO

south • $

Mexican Pacific seafood done Baja California style.

SUERTE

east • $$

The housemade masa is the star at this Mexican-inspired restaurant.

TACODELI

north + central + south + downtown + west • $

Austin's favorite grab & go breakfast taco.

TAMALE HOUSE

east • $

Come for the tamales and stay for the tacos. They still have eight menu items from the original Tamale House of 1958.

TRILL TAQUERIA

east • $

Best gourmet vegetarian tacos served out of a mini trailer.

VALENTINA'S

south • $

Tex-Mex meets barbecue and falls in love at Valentina's.

VAQUERO TAQUERIA

central • $

Authentic breakfast & al pastor street-style tacos. Order the quesadillas (tacos with pan-seared Oaxacan cheese).

VERACRUZ ALL NATURAL

north + south + east • $

And of course, I couldn't leave Veracruz off a best taco list. 71

EL NARANJO

FRESA'S

BEST OF:
MARGARITAS

LA CONDESA

GRIZZELDA'S

EL ALMA
downtown • $$

Extensive list of margaritas on the rocks and frozen, and flavors ranging from simple to spicy to fruity.

EL NARANJO
south lamar • $$

Choose from the classic margarita or create your own for only $2 extra.

FRESA'S
south 1st • $$

The frozen prickly pear margarita with salt is my favorite margarita in the city.

KOKO TIP: The avocado margarita is really good too.

GRIZZELDA'S
east • $$

Eight margaritas to pick from with fun names like Cardi B, Queen Bey, and Cash Money.

GÜERO'S TACO BAR
south congress • $$

Post up on the patio with one of their signature hand-shaken margaritas for prime people-watching on South Congress.

LA CONDESA
downtown • $$

The famed Margarita La Condesa with fresh pineapple juice is another one of my favorite margaritas.

LICHA'S CANTINA
east • $$

If you're looking for quality and quantity, get their margaritas by the glass ($5 during happy hour) or by the pitcher.

MATT'S EL RANCHO
south lamar • $$

Come thirsty—their uber-popular frozen margaritas are served in a sizable glass.

POLVO'S
s. 1st + north + downtown • $$

They do nine different types of margaritas. If you plan on sharing or staying a while, order a pitcher for the table.

TRUDY'S
s. 1st + north + downtown • $$

Talk about a great deal: $4 house margaritas during happy hour and $2.50 ruby red margaritas during brunch until noon.

BEST OF:
QUESO

FRESA'S

EL ALMA
downtown • $$

Order the chile con queso or go for the queso compuesto if you want something meatier.

EL NARANJO
south lamar • $$

Not your basic queso, the queso Oaxaca fundido comes with optional mushrooms, chorizo, or huitlacoche.

FRESA'S
south 1st + south lamar • $$

For a dollar more, you can add chorizo to their classic queso. Or, if you like to go all out, get the Totally Loaded.

GRIZZELDA'S
east • $$

The queso is made with Oaxaca cheese and topped with pickled jalapeños with a side of fresh chips.

GÜERO'S TACO BAR
south congress • $$

I've spent too many afternoons eating queso and drinking margaritas at Güero's.

KOKO TIP: The queso here is great for takeout.

KERBEY LANE CAFE
north + south + east + west + central • $

Kerbey Lane's queso is so out of this world, its recipe literally took a trip to the moon on the SpaceX Falcon 9.

MATT'S EL RANCHO
south lamar • $$

The Bob Armstrong chile con queso is loaded with ground beef, guacamole, sour cream, and pico de gallo.

POLVO'S
s. 1st + north + downtown • $$

Served with bonus ingredients on the side for you to choose what you want to throw in.

TACODELI
north + central + south + west • $

Some days I have the regular queso and other days I have the Roberto's Brazo Fuerte Queso.

TORCHY'S
north + south + east + west + downtown + s. 1st + soco • $

The green chile queso with diablo sauce is a meal in itself.

VERACRUZ ALL NATURAL

FONDA SAN MIGUEL

BEST OF:
MEXICAN

EL NARANJO

SUERTE

ATX COCINA
downtown • $$

Traditional Mexican dishes paired with a drink menu stocked with mezcal and tequila options.

EL NARANJO
south lamar • $$

El Naranjo has raised the bar with their Oaxacan cuisine.

KOKO TIP: Some of the dishes have a spicy kick so my favorite is the mole with duck.

FONDA SAN MIGUEL
central • $$$

You'll feel transported to Mexico from the moment you walk into Fonda San Miguel's hacienda-style space.

HABANERO
south 1st • $

I go here when I'm craving Mexican comfort food.

KOKO TIP: Cash only.

JOE'S BAKERY
east • $

For over 75 years, Joe's Bakery has been a family-run institution serving authentic Mexican breakfast all day and lunch.

LA MEXICANA
south 1st • $

Probaby the cheapest authentic Mexican tacos and pastries in Austin that's open 24/7.

LICHA'S CANTINA
east • $$

Get a taste of inventive Interior Mexico with a margarita.

POLVO'S
downtown + south • $$

Polvo's has stood the Austin test of time, catering to Mexican food and margarita cravings for over 25 years.

SUERTE
east • $$

Masa is the true star at Suerte and you can taste it with the tlacoyos, quesadillas, tostadas, and tacos.

VERACRUZ ALL NATURAL
east + central + north • $

What started as a food truck and has grown into several locations in Austin. All of it is inspired by the city of Veracruz and the tacos, quesadillas, tortas, and aguas frescas live up to its name—all natural.

**BEST OF:
TEX-MEX**

FRESA'S

CHUY'S
north + south • $$

Austin-born Tex-Mex chain started on Barton Springs Road in 1980 and is famous for its "big as yo' face" burritos and the Chicka-Chicka Boom-Boom sauce.

CISCO'S RESTAURANT
east • $

Legendary restaurant that's reminiscent of a classic diner, but with Tex-Mex fare.

EL ALMA
south • $$

Vibrant flavors and rooftop dining with a romantic ambience when the sun sets.

EL CHILE CAFÉ
east • $$

They take all the Tex-Mex staples you know and love and give them a polished element.

FRESA'S
downtown + south 1st • $$

My favorite Tex-Mex spot for its queso, sharable wood-grilled meals, tacos, bols, and margaritas.

GRIZZELDA'S
east • $$

Colorful Tex-Mex restaurant with a very Instagrammable bright pink wall outside.

GÜERO'S TACO BAR
south congress • $$

Come for the tacos, queso, and margaritas, and stay for the live music and more margaritas.

JUAN IN A MILLION
east • $

Hands down the best deal in town for a down-home Tex-Mex breakfast.

LA CONDESA
downtown • $$

You won't find queso or enchiladas but order the guacamole sampler, tacos, ceviches, and Tex-Mex plates and you won't miss them.

MATT'S EL RANCHO
south lamar • $$

Sizzling fajitas, burritos, flautas, enchiladas, and chile rellenos in a family-friendly setting since 1952.

TEX-MEX

VALENTINA'S

LA BARBECUE

**BEST OF:
BARBECUE**

RUDY'S

KERLIN BBQ

BLACK'S BARBECUE
central • $$

Three generations of the Black Family have been serving barbecue with locations in Lockhart, New Braunfels, San Marcos, and Austin.

FRANKLIN BARBECUE
east • $$

If there's any place that you're going to wait 3+ hours, Franklin Barbecue is it.

KOKO TIP: Preorder in advance and pick up (five pounds of meat minimum).

KERLIN BBQ
east • $

Solid pick for brisket, brisket kolaches, ribs, sausage, and sides without the wait.

LA BARBECUE
east • $$

My no. 1 barbecue spot in Austin with fall-off-the-bone dinosaur-sized beef ribs.

LEROY & LEWIS
south congress • $$

This food truck smokes specialty meats like beef cheeks and Akaushi brisket.

MICKLETHWAIT
east • $$

Come for the brisket, ribs, and sausage and stay for the sides and desserts.

THE SALT LICK
north + southwest • $$

I love The Salt Lick because their meat pit is such a sight to see with all the hanging meats. Plus it's all-you-can-eat and BYOB.

STILES SWITCH BBQ
central • $$

St. Louis-style pork ribs, pulled pork, smoked chicken, sausage, and Bloody Marys made with the barbecue sauce.

RUDY'S
north + central + west • $

This Texas-original chain is one my bbq favorites for its moist brisket, creamed corn, and banana pudding.

VALENTINA'S
south • $$

You can have both Tex-Mex and barbecue at this food trailer.

BARBECUE

BEST OF:
ASIAN

JAPANESE

- Daruma Ramen $$
- DipDipDip $$$
- East Side King $
- Fukumoto $$
- Kemuri Tatsu-Ya $$
- Komé $
- Kura Revolving Sushi $
- Kyōten Sushiko $$
- Ni-Komé $$
- Otoko $$$$
- Ramen Tatsu-Ya $
- Soto $$
- Uchi $$$
- Uchiko $$$
- Uroko $

CHINESE

- 101 By Teahaus $
- Asia Cafe $
- Coco's Cafe $
- Jade Restaurant $$
- Julie's Noodles $
- Lin Asian Bar $$
- New Fortune $
- Old Thousand $$
- Rice Bowl Cafe $
- Sugar Pine $
- Wu Chow $$

VIETNAMESE

- 888 Pan Asian $
- Baguette House $
- Elizabeth St. Cafe $$
- Pho Please $
- Pho Dan $
- Pho Saigon $

KOREAN

- Charm Korean BBQ $$
- Chi'Lantro BBQ $
- College Roadhouse $
- Korea House $
- Oseyo $$

THAI

- DEE DEE $
- Madam Mam's $
- Sap's Fine Thai Cuisine $
- Sway $$$
- Thai Fresh $$
- Thai Kun $$
- Titaya's $

FILIPINO

- Be More Pacific $

INDIAN

- G'raj Mahal $$
- Nasha $

**BEST OF:
KID-FRIENDLY**

HAT CREEK BURGER

CENTRAL MARKET
central + southwest • $

Shaded playground, cafe with a kids menu, and live music on most weekends. Free kids' entree with the purchase of an adult entree on Tuesdays after 5pm.

HAT CREEK BURGER
north + central + southwest • $

Fun and open outdoor playground, kids' menu, and build-your-own milkshakes. Half off the Little Hat, Big Hat, or Signature burger on Tuesdays after 5pm.

HOME SLICE PIZZA
central + south congress • $

Pizza isn't a hard sell for kids, and they give your little ones raw dough to play with.

JACOBY'S
east • $$

Kids eat free on Sunday nights & there's a massive backyard.

KERBEY LANE CAFE
north + south + east + west + central • $

Kids eat free all day on Tuesdays with the purchase of an adult entree.

LUCY'S FRIED CHICKEN
central + south congress + west • $$

The location on the lake has an outdoor play area for kids and outdoor seating for you.

MANDOLA'S
north + central + southwest + west • $$

Outdoor playscape at all three of their locations. Kid entrees come with a soft drink and a scoop of gelato.

PHIL'S ICEHOUSE
north + central + s lamar • $

Play area outside, awesome kids' menu inside, and Amy's ice cream right next door.

SKI SHORES CAFE
west • $

If the playground and sandpit aren't enough, you'll love family movie night with free s'mores for the kiddos.

WATERLOO ICE HOUSE
north + south + west + southwest • $$

A popular gathering spot for a kids' playdate, thanks to their spacious shaded playground and coloring menu.

CHEER UP CHARLIES

STUBB'S

STUBBS

TUE SLAYYYTER
WED JAM FOR HAAM
THU HOLY WAVE
SUN GOSPEL BRUNC

**BEST OF:
LIVE MUSIC**

hotel

Mohawk

COCKTAILS

Mohawk

THE ROOSEVELT ROOM

MOHAWK

ACL LIVE
downtown

Home to Austin City Limits, ACL Live is the longest running music series in American TV history and puts on 100 concerts a year.

ANTONE'S
downtown

Iconic blues venue established in 1975 that used to be a playground for Stevie Ray Vaughan and other music legends.

CHEER UP CHARLIES
downtown

Colorful, queer-friendly, and vegan, this intimate venue specializes in fun DJ sets and funky dance music.

ELEPHANT ROOM
downtown

This underground jazz lounge on Congress Ave. is a hidden gem.

EMO'S
south

Emo's helped define Austin's live music scene as host to many bands in the punk and rock 'n' roll genre.

MOHAWK AUSTIN
downtown

Music/event venue where you can catch a live show nearly every night.

PARISH
downtown

Indoor live music venue with hip-hop, rock, funk, reggae, Latin, and more. Best known for their booming sound system.

HISTORIC SCOOT INN
east

One of Austin's original venues, opened in 1955 and puts on lots of free shows.

STUBB'S BAR-B-Q
downtown

Entirely outdoor amphitheater that makes big headliners seem like they're putting on intimate shows. Eat at Stubbs on Sunday mornings to catch the Gospel Brunch.

THE ROOSEVELT ROOM
downtown

Sip on inventive craft cocktails while listening to live music every Thursday.

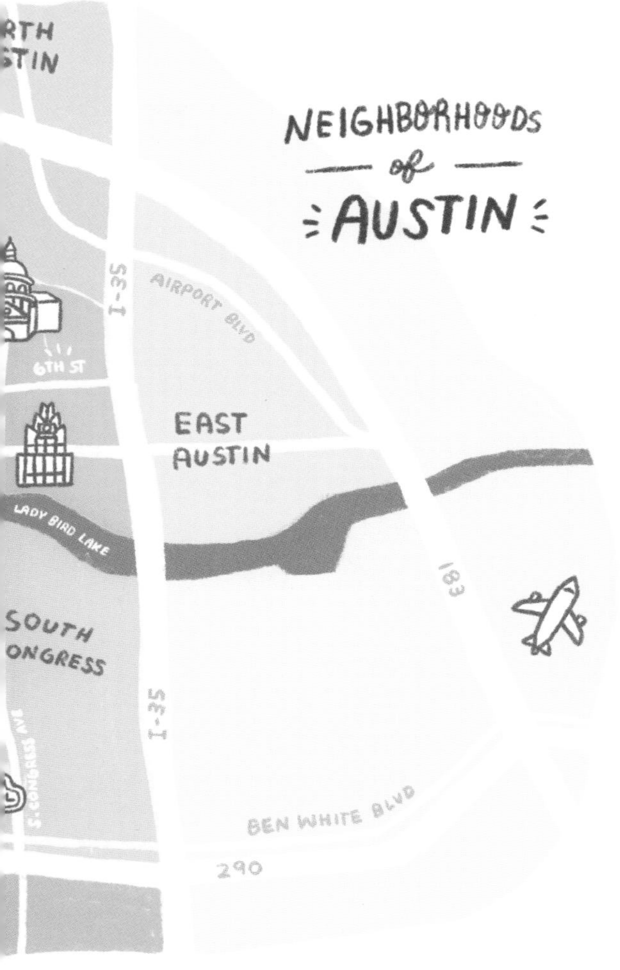

NEIGHBORHOODS
— of —
≳ AUSTIN ≲

RTH
STIN

I-35

AIRPORT BLVD

6TH ST

EAST
AUSTIN

LADY BIRD LAKE

183

SOUTH
CONGRESS

I-35

S. CONGRESS AVE

BEN WHITE BLVD

290

AUSTIN BEERWORKS

ASIA MARKET

BEST OF:
NORTH
AUSTIN

RAMEN TATSU-YA

SWA

COFFEE

CRAFTWORK COFFEE CO.
coffee shop with a private
coworking space

EPOCH COFFEE
24/7 coffee shop

SUMMER MOON
wood-fired, fair trade coffee shop
famous for its Moon Milk

HOUNDSTOOTH
contemporary coffee shop with
carefully crafted coffee & craft
cocktails

BREAKFAST

TACODELI
Austin's favorite breakfast tacos

JUICELAND
fresh juice & smoothie shop

KERBEY LANE CAFE
beloved Austin cafe that has
breakfast, lunch, and dinner 24/7

BIDERMAN'S BAGELS
casual Jewish-style cafe with
bagels and deli sandwiches

VERACRUZ ALL NATURAL
authentic breakfast tacos, picadas
(open-faced tacos), smoothies, and
more in a brick-and-mortar space

LUNCH

CHUY'S
local Tex-Mex restaurant chain with
Elvis-themed decor

CHI'LANTRO BBQ
Korean-Mexican fusion tacos, bowls,
and kimchi fries

COCO'S CAFE
Taiwanese cafe with rice and noodle
plates and bubble tea

BAGUETTE HOUSE
my favorite Vietnamese bánh mì shop

HONEST MARY'S
healthy restaurant with build-your-
own grain bowls

STILES SWITCH BBQ
St. Louis-style pork ribs, pulled pork,
smoked chicken, and Bloody Marys

BE MORE PACIFIC
Filipino restaurant with creative &
classic dishes

TOMODACHI SUSHI
don't underestimate this sushi spot
in the strip mall, the owners used to
work at Nobu Las Vegas

DINNER

ANDIAMO RESTAURANTE
authentic Italian restaurant with
Italian wines

ASIA CAFE
authentic Chinese restaurant with
generous portions

CHARM KOREAN BBQ
all-you-can-eat Korean bbq

GARBO'S LOBSTER
New England favorites like fresh
oysters, lobster rolls, clam chowder,
and fish & chips

PHO DAN
my favorite spot for pho

RAMEN TATSU-YA
OG location of the popular Japanese
ramen restaurant

RICE BOWL CAFE
authentic Chinese food

SWAY
fine-dining Thai restaurant

DESSERT

CHOCOLATERIE TESSA
local chocolaterie that makes
specialty chocolates, truffles, and
caramels

HAY ELOTES
Mexican elotes, street snacks, and
fruit cups

SNOMO
Taiwanese shaved ice and
bubble tea

BARS & BREWERIES

AUSTIN BEERWORKS
Austin craft brewery with IPAs & ales

77° ROOFTOP PATIO BAR
fancy rooftop bar with a
hookah lounge

KUNG FU SALOON
vintage arcade bar known for their
signature saké bombs and Skee-Ball

WONDER BAR
fun bar with Instagrammable
installations

HAPPY HOUR

ELDORADO CAFÉ
Tuesday to Friday, 4-6pm

JACK ALLEN'S KITCHEN
Monday to Friday, 3-7pm
half off appetizers plus drink specials

THAI KUN
Monday to Friday, 5-7pm
discounted snacks & drinks

SALT TRADER'S
Monday, 3:30-10pm
Tuesday to Friday, 3:30-6:30pm

SECOND BAR + KITCHEN
daily happy hour, 3-6pm

SWAY
Monday to Friday, 3-6pm
half off specialty cocktails, wines,
sake, & beer

SHOPS

ERIN CONDREN
colorful stationery, notebooks &
planners

LIMBO
handmade jewelry & local gift shop

LUXE APOTHETIQUE
trendy gift shop with women's
clothing, beauty, and fun gifts

NINA BERENATO JEWELRY
edgy, handmade, and sustainable
jewelry shop

W3LL PEOPLE
clean, plant-based beauty

HANK'S

UNCLE NICKY'S

BEST OF:
CENTRAL
AUSTIN

BATCH

THE PEACHED TORTILLA

COFFEE

EASY TIGER
bake shop and beer garden

CAFFÉ MEDICI
Austin's original specialty coffee shop

HANK'S
beautifully designed coffee shop and
cafe with an outdoor patio

HALCYON
coffee, caffeinated cocktails, and
table top s'mores

PACHA
this tiny coffee shop serves organic
and locally sourced coffee

SA-TÉN
Japanese coffeehouse with breakfast,
lunch, and dinner

BREAKFAST

AÇAÍ HUT
açaí bowls & Brazilian cheese bread

**BATCH CRAFT BEER
& KOLACHES**
homemade kolaches and huge
selection of canned beer

ÉPICERIE
French-American cafe with beignets

KERBEY LANE CAFE
beloved 24/7 Austin cafe that has
breakfast, lunch, and dinner

NERVOUS CHARLIE'S
New York City-style bagels

TEXAS FRENCH BREAD
farm-to-table bakery and cafe

THE STEEPING ROOM
tea shop with a healthy menu

UPPER CRUST BAKERY
European bakery with made-from-
scratch pastries

UNCLE NICKY'S
all-day cafe in Hyde Park inspired
by northern Italian cafes

LUNCH

AVENUE B GROCERY
Austin's oldest grocery store and has
sandwiches

COLLEEN'S KITCHEN
Southern-inspired chic restaurant
and bar

EAST SIDE PIES
thin crust pizza shop that's popular
for delivery

FRICANO'S DELI
sandwich shop near UT campus

HOME SLICE PIZZA
NY-style pizza by the slice or pie with
a walk-up window

HYDE PARK BAR & GRILL
neighborhood restaurant known for
its batter-dipped French fries

JOSEPHINE HOUSE
New American cottage with a cute,
airy patio

MEZZEME
Turkish Mediterranean rice bowls,
salads, and pitas

NAU'S ENFIELD DRUG
Austin's only original full-service soda
fountain pharmacy since 1951

OTHERSIDE DELI
really good pastrami sandwiches

PICNIK
healthy cafe with vegan, vegetarian, and paleo options

PHIL'S ICEHOUSE
hearty burger joint with shakes

SOUP PEDDLER
homemade soups and grilled cheeses

TUMBLE 22
Nashville-style hot chicken

VAQUERO TAQUERO
authentic Mexican street-style taco spot that specializes in al pastor

VIA 313
Detroit-style pizza (extra thick & crispy crust)

DINNER

CIPOLLINA
Italian restaurant with handmade pastas and wood-fired pizzas

DIPDIPDIP
fancy shabu-shabu dining experience

FONDA SAN MIGUEL
traditional Mexican restaurant

FOREIGN & DOMESTIC
farm-to-table neighborhood spot

JEFFREY'S
swanky, upscale New American restaurant for steaks and caviar

KOMÉ
contemporary Japanese restaurant with sushi & homey Japanese dishes

MANDOLA'S ITALIAN
family-friendly Italian restaurant with an Italian market and gelato

OLIVE & JUNE
Southern Italian cuisine in a three-story treehouse

OLAMAIE
Southern restaurant known for its famous off-the-menu biscuits

THE PEACHED TORTILLA
elevated Asian comfort food

TITAYA'S
authentic Thai restaurant

HAPPY HOUR

BARLEY SWINE
Sunday to Friday, 5-6:30pm

CONTIGO
Monday to Friday, 5-6:30pm

PICNIK
Monday to Friday, 3-6pm

L'OCA D'ORO
every day until 6:30pm

THE PEACHED TORTILLA
daily in the bar area, 5-7pm

DESSERT

CASEY'S NEW ORLEANS SNOWBALLS
family-owned snowball stand since 1996

CHURRO CO.
fresh, hot churros topped with ice cream & more

FLUFF MERINGUES & MORE
meringue dessert shop

LADY QUACKENBUSH'S
pastel-hued bakery and coffee shop

KELLIE'S BAKING CO.
bakery with edible Instabite
photo-printed cookies

MRS. JOHNSON'S BAKERY
drive-thru donut shop since 1948

LA PÂTISSERIE
French bake shop with macarons

LICK HONEST ICE CREAMS
ice cream shop with artisanal scoops

TINY PIES
tiny pie shop

SWEET RITUAL
vegan ice cream shop

BARS & BREWERIES

B.D. RILEY'S IRISH PUB
Irish bar with Guinness pours

DRAUGHT HOUSE PUB
brewpub with 70+ craft beers

EASY TIGER
bake shop & beer garden

HOPFIELDS
gastropub with French-inspired fare

LALA'S
dive bar with yr-round holiday decor

TEXAS SAKÉ COMPANY
Texas saké taproom with saké on tap,
by the flight, and by the bottle

SHOPS

ADELANTE
chic women's apparel & accessories

ANTONELLI'S CHEESE SHOP
artisanal speciality cheese shop with
cheese pairing classes

ATOWN
local gift shop with souvenirs of Austin

AUSTIN FLOWER CO.
flower shop with plants and stems

FRESH PLUS GROCERY
local Austin grocery store since 1927

HEARTH & SOUL
lifestyle shop of clothes, accessories,
home decor, books, and more

I LUV VIDEO
one of the world's oldest video stores

MAGIC CARAVAN
Turkish vintage rug shop

RABBIT FOOD GROCERY
friendly vegan grocery store

SHOAL CREEK NURSERY
giant garden center

SLEDD'S NURSERY
indoor/outdoor nursery in Clarksville

SOUTHERN HIPPIE
women's boutique with Australian
brands

SUCCULENT NATIVE
succulent & houseplant boutique

WOOD & ROSE
curated women's clothing store

KERLIN BBQ

TAMALE HOUSE

¡HOLA!

Tamale House

ESTABLISHED 1938 · AUSTIN-TEX

**BEST OF:
EAST AUSTIN**

EAST AUSTIN SUCCULE

KEMURI TATSU-YA

COFFEE

CENOTE
coffee shop in a circa 1887
bungalow house

CUVÉE COFFEE
coffee roaster with pour-overs,
espresso, and nitrogenated cold
brews on tap

GREATER GOODS
coffee shop in a converted
automotive warehouse

FLEET COFFEE
tiny coffee shop with classic &
creative coffee drinks

FLAT TRACK COFFEE
coffee shop with a bike shop

HOUNDSTOOTH
contemporary coffee shop with
carefully crafted coffee

THUNDERBIRD COFFEE
love honey nut latte and Thai iced
coffee

SA-TÉN COFFEE
Japanese coffeehouse with breakfast,
lunch, and dinner

**WRIGHT BROS. BREW
AND BREW**
coffee and craft brews in an
industrial space

BREAKFAST

BIRD BIRD BISCUIT
freshly made-to-order biscuit
breakfast sandwich shop

BLENDERS & BOWLS
açaí bowls and smoothies made with
superfood ingredients

CISCO'S RESTAURANT
Tex-Mex diner that's been recognized
as a historic landmark

HILLSIDE FARMACY
New American restaurant that
focuses on locally sourced ingredients
in a historic 1950s pharmacy

JOE'S BAKERY
family-run restaurant that serves an
authentic Mexican breakfast all day
and lunch

JUAN IN A MILLION
Mexican restaurant with the cheapest
and most generous Tex-Mex
breakfast portions

PAPERBOY
cute pink food trailer that serves
breakfast and lunch

VERACRUZ ALL NATURAL
authentic Mexican restaurant & trailer
that makes the best migas tacos

LUNCH

BLUE DAHLIA BISTRO
light and airy European-inspired cafe

BUENOS AIRES CAFÉ
authentic Argentinian restaurant

DAI DUE
butcher shop that serves a
farm-to-table menu

DISCADA
trailer serving northern Mexican
discada tacos

CASA COLOMBIA
South American Colombian restaurant

EL CHILITO
colorful taco stand that's popular for takeout

FRANKLIN BARBECUE
famous barbecue restaurant with long lines

KINDA TROPICAL
retro plant-filled all-day cafe and grocery

LA BARBECUE
my favorite barbecue spot in Austin for its brisket and beef ribs

LA MATTA
Italian sandwich shop with charcuterie boards

MICKLETHWAIT CRAFT MEATS
barbecue trailer with sides & desserts

TAMALE HOUSE
Mexican restaurant known for its breakfast tacos, migas, and tamales

RAMEN TATSU-YA
best ramen in Austin

UROKO
tiny Japanese restaurant that makes handrolls during the day & omakase on the weekends

DINNER

BUFALINA
Neapolitan pizza restaurant

EL CHILE CAFÉ Y CANTINA
puffy tacos and margaritas

FUKUMOTO SUSHI
Japanese izakaya with traditional sushi and yakitori

GRIZZELDA'S
cute Tex-Mex restaurant with an Instagrammable pink wall

INTERO
Farm-to-table Italian pasta, entrees, and artisanal chocolate

IL BRUTTO
I like coming here for the wood-grilled pizza and an Aperol Spritz

JACOBY'S
farm-to-ranch restaurant, backyard garden, and shop

JUSTINE'S BRASSERIE
French food and cocktails in a bungalow space and light-strung patio

KEMURI TATSU-YA
izakaya & bar with Japanese & Texas influences

MI MADRE'S RESTAURANT
botanas, tacos, burritos, & platos fuertes

LAUNDERETTE
classy New American restaurant in a converted laundromat

PATRIZI'S
food trailer that makes homemade Italian pasta

ROSEWOOD
South Texas cuisine in a historic 1890s home

OLD THOUSAND
Chinese food & craft cocktails in a hipster space

OSEYO
traditional Korean food &
cocktails in a chic space

SUERTE
contemporary Mexican food that
focuses on masa

YUYO
bright Peruvian restaurant

HAPPY HOUR

BARZÓN
Wednesday to Friday, 5-7pm

GRIZZELDA'S
Tuesday to Friday, 5-7pm

EL CHILE Y CAFÉ
every day, 3-6:30pm

EASTSIDE TAVERN
Monday to Friday, 3-6pm

FUKUMOTO
Monday to Thursday, 5–6:30pm

NASHA
Monday to Friday, 4-7pm

LAUNDRETTE
Monday to Friday, 5-6pm

LICHA'S CANTINA
Tuesday to Friday, 4-6pm

TAKOBA
Wednesday to Friday, 4-6pm

YUYO
all night on Monday and Tuesday
Wednesday to Sunday, 4:30-6:30pm

DESSERT

AMY'S ICE CREAM
Austin's beloved ice cream shop

CAPITAL CITY BAKERY
vegan bakery with cupcakes, cookies,
& cakes

GELATERIA GEMELLI
modern gelato shop & Italian cocktail
bar

PROHIBITION CREAMERY
boozy ice cream shop with cocktails

SPUN ICE CREAM
liquid nitrogen ice cream shop

SUGAR MAMA'S
cupcakes & cake shop

BARS

AH SING DEN
Asian-themed bar named after the
owner of one of East London's most
famous opium dens with really good
tipples & morsels

KOKO TIP: Cool spot for brunch.

BARZÓN
Mexican bar with Mexican food

DOMO ALLEY-GATO
Japanese bar that serves curries and
other bar food

GRACKLE
hipster bar with a pool table, billiards,
and jukebox

KITTY COHEN'S
retro bar with 1970s Palm Springs
vibes and a mini pool

NATIVE HOSTEL
cool, modern hostel with a kitchen
& bar

LAST STRAW
tiki bar with vacation vibes

KOKO TIP: If you're hungry, the food
menu is pretty good.

LUSTRE PEARL
chill hangout spot for drinks

NICKEL CITY
retro watering hole with a coney dog
food truck

STAY GOLD
hip bar & lounge with live music

SHANGRI-LA
bar with a dog-friendly patio & beer
garden

THE LIBERTY
one of the oldest bars on East 6th
& the East Side King food trailer is
parked in the back

THE WHITE HORSE
honky-tonk bar with live country
music

THE VORTEX
artist owned theatre that produces
original & non-traditional theatre
works

WHISLER'S
one of my favorite spots for craft
cocktails

KOKO TIP: Head up the stairs for the
mezcal bar.

BREWERIES

BLUE OWL BREWING
first brewery in Austin to create sour
mash

HOPS AND GRAIN BREWING
craft beer microbrewery with a
taproom & tours

LAZARUS BREWING CO
bright blue colored brewery and
coffee shop

ZILKER BREWING CO
urban craft brewery & taproom with
the Spicy Boys food truck

SHOPS

AMANDA DEER JEWELRY
local shop with dainty, everyday
jewelry

AUSTIN PLANT SUPPLY
plant shop with plants of all sizes &
species

APT F
handmade and ethically sourced
home goods shop with vintage rugs

ARO
curated collection of women's
clothing, jewelry, & accessories

CHARM SCHOOL VINTAGE
women's vintage clothing shop

COCO COQUETTE
pick up a wig or host a wig party with
friends at this wig shop

KOKO TIP: Fun bachlorette activity!
Pick out a new 'do and rock it on Dirty
6th or Rainey Street.

EAST AUSTIN SUCCULENTS
cactus & succulent nursery heaven for every #plantlady

KOKO TIP: Cool spot for engagement photos. Book in advance online.

EA/ST CO.
curated home goods shop by design and craftsmanship

HELM BOOTS
flagship store for handmade leather boot brand for men & women

HOUSE OF ST. CLAIR
contemporary men's fashion clothing and lifestyle shop

KAMMOCK
outdoor sports store for adventure takers

KEITH KREEGER
handmade porcelain ceramics for restaurants and homes

KOKO TIP: Dine on his plates at Uchi, Uchiko, and Emmer & Rye.

MANA CULTURE
boho chic clothing & jewelry shop

MIRANDA BENNETT STUDIO
modern, plant-dyed, and sustainably made apparel

PLANT PARTY
houseplant shop that offers build-your-own terrarium parties

SOLID GOLD
women's boutique with clothing, jewelry, & home goods

SON OF A SAILOR
handmade jewelry & leather goods

THE PAPER + CRAFT PANTRY
stationery store & workshop studio

THE BEE GROCERY
local urban grocer with fresh & prepared foods and household necessities

TILLERY STREET PLANT CO.
nursery with succulents and tropical houseplants

TAKE HEART
one of my favorite gift shops in Austin for handmade home goods

STAY

ARRIVE EAST AUSTIN HOTEL
- 83 guest rooms
- rooms start at $199
- coffee shop, restaurant, & two bars

EAST AUSTIN HOTEL
- 75 guest rooms
- rooms start at $99
- all-day cafe, rooftop bar, pool, & pool bar

HEYWOOD HOTEL
- 7 guest rooms
- rooms start at $199
- free parking & free bikes

HOTEL ELEVEN
- 14 guest rooms
- rooms start at $199
- lounge & rooftop deck

NATIVE HOSTEL
- 12 guest rooms with 66 beds
- beds start at $49
- coffee shop, restaurant, & bar

JO'S COFFEE

ATX COCINA

BEST OF:
DOWNTOWN

LA CONDESA

LE POLITIQUE

COFFEE

CAFFÉ MEDICI
this location has a great view of downtown Austin from the second floor

BETTER HALF
stellar coffee, draft cocktails, wine, beer, and food

JUAN PELOTA
coffee shop connected to Mellow Johnny's bike shop that's owned by Lance Armstrong

JO'S COFFEE
every Tuesday from 5-8pm is two-for-one burgers

MERIT COFFEE
coffee shop from San Antonio with fresh pastries

BREAKFAST

1886 CAFÉ & BAKERY
Victorian-style cafe in the historic Driskill Hotel

BLENDERS AND BOWLS
healthy açaí cafe located inside Wanderlust Yoga

HIGH NOTE
healthy all-day restaurant & bar with healthy cocktails

WALTON'S FANCY & STAPLE
bakery and flower shop with classic breakfast options like avocado toast and shrimp & grits

LUNCH

40 NORTH
neighborhood Neapolitan pizza spot

COOKBOOK BAR & CAFÉ
located in the Austin Central Library with a menu from influential cookbooks

FAREGROUND
Austin's first food hall with six restaurants & two bars

SECOND BAR + KITCHEN
hearty salads, sandwiches, pizza, cocktails, and wines by the glass

SWIFT'S ATTIC
great lunch deal where you can get a sandwich with fries, cup of soup, or side salad for under $14

TRACE
Lunch on the Fly deal is only $13 for a three-course meal with complimentary valet on the weekdays

DINNER

ARLO GREY
lakeview restaurant inside the LINE Austin hotel

ATX COCINA
upscale modern Mexican restaurant

COMEDOR
modern Mexican restaurant that brings a taste of Mexico City

ITALIC
downtown Italian restaurant with pasta, wood-fired pizza, and Italian wines

LA CONDESA
one of my favorite modern
Mexican restaurants

LAMBERTS
fancy barbecue restaurant

LE POLITIQUE
fine dining French restaurant and
coffee shop

THE BACKSPACE
intimate pizza restaurant that makes
thin-crust Neapolitan pies

THE DRISKILL GRILL
iconic steakhouse inside The Driskill
Hotel

SHE'S NOT HERE
Japanese restaurant with Thai &
Hawaiian influences

MOONSHINE BAR & GRILL
Southern comfort food served in a
historic home from the mid-1850s

WU CHOW
modern Chinese food + tiki drinks

HAPPY HOUR

ATX COCINA
every day, 4:30-6pm

FIXE
Monday to Saturday, 4:30-7pm
Sunday, 2pm-close

HOLY ROLLER
all day Tuesday
Monday to Friday, 4-7pm

IRENE'S
Monday to Saturday, 3-6:30pm
Sunday, 10am-12pm

ITALIC
Monday to Friday, 2:30-6:30pm
Sunday, 10am-12pm

PARKSIDE
every day, 5-6pm
half off the entire menu

RED ASH
every day, 4:30-6:30pm
discounted appetizers & $2 off all
cocktails, beer & wine

DESSERTS

FROZEN ROLLS CREAMERY
Thai-rolled ice cream shop

JIM-JIM'S WATER ICE
real-fruit-flavored Italian ice shop

LA CAFÉ CRÊPE
French sweet and savory crêpes,
coffee, beer, and wine

BARS & BREWERIES

CENTRAL DISTRICT BREWING
women-led, small-batch brewery

ELLIS
sleek cocktail bar and patio at
Fareground

FLOPPY DISK REPAIR CO
secret speakeasy that requires a
door code

KOKO TIP: Ask the bartenders at
HandleBar for the code.

GARAGE
secret bar hidden in a parking
garage

HANDLEBAR
bar near Dirty 6th with a rooftop view

HANGAR LOUNGE
upscale bar and lounge with DJs &
buzzy rooftop

HERE NOR THERE
secret speakeasy that requires
reservations via an app

LIVING ROOM
sexy cocktail bar at the W Austin Hotel

MIDNIGHT COWBOY
secret bar that requires reservations
in advance via the website

P6
rooftop bar at the LINE Austin hotel
with the best view of Lady Bird Lake

PÉCHÉ
Austin's first absinthe bar with
pre-prohibition style cocktails

SMALL VICTORY
secret bar with a serious cocktail &
ice program

THE ROOSEVELT ROOM
award-winning, 1920s-inspired
cocktail bar

SHOPS

AUSTIN ROCKS
apparel, gifts, & souvenir gift shop

BOOKPEOPLE
locally owned bookstore in Austin &
the largest bookstore in Texas

LUXE APOTHETIQUE
trendy gift shop that sells women's
clothing & fun gifts

ROYAL BLUE GROCERY
modern urban grocery store with
Stumptown coffee

THOM'S MARKET
local grocery store with breakfast
tacos, coffee, wine, and Texas beers

TOY JOY
unique toy store for both kids & adults

STAY

HOTEL VAN ZANDT
- 319 guest rooms (41 suites &
  5 presidential suites)
- rooms start at $170
- cafe with coffee bar, restaurant,
  bar, & rooftop pool
- dog-friendly

THE DRISKILL HOTEL
- oldest operating hotel in Austin
  since 1886
- 189 guest rooms
- rooms start at $159
- cafe, restaurant, & bar
- live music every night & monthly
- Victorian afternoon tea service
- dog-friendly

WESTIN
- 366 guest rooms (4 suites)
- rooms start at $260
- restaurant, rooftop pool, & bar
- dog-friendly

W HOTEL
- 251 guest rooms
- rooms start at $229
- restaurant, spa, bar, & pool
- dog-friendly

JO'S COFFEE

HOME SLICE PIZZA

BEST OF: SOUTH CONGRESS

AUSTIN MOTEL

WILLIE FOR PRESIDENT MURAL

COFFEE

COSMIC COFFEE
coffee shop & beer garden with a big backyard

MAÑANA
chic coffee shop at South Congress Hotel with housemade pastries

JO'S COFFEE
walk-up coffee shop with the iconic I Love You So Much mural

TOMS ROASTING CO
TOMS footwear has their own coffee shop in Austin

BREAKFAST

CAFÉ NO SÉ
all-day cafe located inside South Congress Hotel

MAGNOLIA CAFE
24-hour cafe loved for its breakfast, Tex-Mex, & pancakes

JOANN'S FINE FOODS
stylish, 60s-mod diner connected to the Austin Motel

JUNE'S ALL DAY
chic cafe & wine bar

SOUTH CONGRESS CAFE
daily brunch & drink specials at this retro cafe

LUNCH

BURRO CHEESE KITCHEN
gourmet grilled cheese sandwiches served from a shipping container

HOME SLICE PIZZA
NY-style pizza by the slice or pie with a walk-up window

HOPDODDY
burger joint known for its all-natural meat patties, housemade buns, & shakes

KOKO TIP: I usually order the Prime-time burger or Impossible™ burger.

LUCKY ROBOT
Japanese restaurant focused on Tokyo-style street food & sustainable sushi

TORCHY'S TACOS
Torchy's flagship location that serves the same iconic tacos & margaritas

VINAIGRETTE
really big, hearty salads & healthy cocktails

DINNER

LEROY AND LEWIS BARBECUE
smoked meat food truck specializing in unusual cuts of meats & side dishes

OTOKO
12-seat Japanese omakase restaurant

PERLA'S
fancy seafood restaurant with the best people-watching patio

THAI FRESH
authentic Thai dishes, homemade ice creams, & gluten-free bakery

VESPAIO
my favorite spot for fresh Italian pasta

HAPPY HOUR

COSMIC COFFEE
Sunday to Thursday, 9pm-close

Monday: $6 Lone Star + shot of Tullamore Dew or Pacifico + shot of Arrette Tequila

Tuesday: $3 Pacifico or Arette Tequila & $5 palomas

Wednesday: $5 glasses of wine

Thursday: $5 frozen cocktails

CENTRAL STANDARD
Monday to Friday, 3–6:30pm
Half off the full beverage menu including beer, wines by the bottle and glass, house cocktails, and $3 East Coast oysters

HOPDODDY
Monday to Friday, 3–6:30pm
$5 Continental Club burger, select craft drafts, all wine, starts, & boozy drinks

LUCKY ROBOT
Monday to Friday, 4:30-6pm
Half price appetizers and select bottles of sake & wine, and $5 & under Lucky bites

SOCO HOTEL LOBBY BAR
Monday to Friday, 5-7pm

BARS

COSMIC COFFEE
local beers & craft cocktails

WATERTRADE
hidden Japanese cocktail bar at the South Congress Hotel

VELOURIA
coffee shop during the day & cocktail bar at night

DESSERTS

AMY'S ICE CREAM
order scoops of ice cream & milkshakes from the walk-up window

BIG TOP CANDY SHOP
whimsical circus-themed candy shop

HEY CUPCAKE!
airstream trailer that serves cupcakes

HOWDY DONUT
tiny donut shop with kolaches & really good donuts

SHOPS

ALLENS BOOTS
iconic store in Austin with more than 4,000 boots

BY GEORGE
high-end women's and men's boutique with designer clothing & accessories

CO-STAR
hip women's & men's clothing store with designer finds

COVE
trendy women's clothing shop in a bright space

KENDRA SCOTT
fashion & fine jewelry shop with home decor & beauty

LITTLE LIMBO
super cute shop with children's toys & gifts, and Instagrammable mural outside

LIMBO JEWELRY
modern, architectural gold & silver jewelry

MAYA STAR
women's clothing & jewelry store

PARTS & LABOUR
gift shop with handmade gifts exclusively from Texas-based artists

PRIMA DORA
local gift shop that celebrates that authentic small town "Old Austin" vibe with local artist goods

RIVERCITY MARKET
go-to shop for snacks, coffee, tacos, sandwiches, beer & wine

STAG PROVISIONS FOR MEN
trendy men's boutique with classic and modern styles

SOUTH CONGRESS BOOKS
small bookstore with used, collectible, & unique books

SUNROOM
women's clothing store inspired by the West Coast & urban sensibility

STAY

AUSTIN MOTEL
- 41 guest rooms
- rooms start at $120
- restaurant & pool
- dog-friendly

HOTEL SAN JOSÉ
- 40 guest rooms
- rooms start at $190
- courtyard & pool
- dog-friendly

HOTEL SAINT CECILIA
- 14 guest rooms
- rooms start at $500
- lounge, pool, & Shinola bikes
- dog-friendly

SOUTH CONGRESS HOTEL
- 71 guest rooms, 10 suites, & 2 suites
- rooms start at $190
- three restaurants, coffee shop, pool, bar, and lobby bar
- dog-friendly

MURALS

I LOVE YOU SO MUCH
1300 South Congress Ave.

Hotelier Liz Lambert and musician Amy Cook were drunk, got into a fight, and broke up. Amy spray-painted "I love you so much" on the side of Jo's Coffee so Liz could see it when she opened up the next day. The couple has been together ever since.

LOVE FROM AUSTIN
1912 South Congress Ave.

WILLIE FOR PRESIDENT
1315 South Congress Ave.

LITTLE LIMBO
1700 South Congress Ave.

SOUTH CONGRESS MURAL
1800 South Congress Ave.

ROADHOUSE RELICS

GREETINGS FROM AUSTIN MURAL

Roadhouse RELICS
ART GALLERY & GIFTS

GREETINGS FROM AUSTIN
Capitol OF TEXAS

**BEST OF:
SOUTH 1ST**

DOLCE

1713

DOLCE NEVE

PLANTS

FROND PLANT SHOP

COFFEE

ONCE OVER COFFEE
neighborhood coffee shop with a
back deck

SEVENTH FLAG COFFEE
coffee shop with living room vibes

SUMMER MOON
wood-fired, fair-trade hand-roasted
coffee shop

KOKO TIP: I like the Half Moon
during the winter time.

BREAKFAST

BOULDIN CREEK CAFE
eco-friendly vegetarian restaurant

EL PRIMO
Mexican street taco food stand

KOKO TIP: Don't miss the homemade
hot sauce in the squeeze bottles.

LA MEXICANA BAKERY
24/7 hole-in-the-wall Mexican
restaurant & bakery

KOKO TIP: They usually fry up
churros after midnight.

PHOEBE'S DINER
vintage diner that serves breakfast,
brunch, & lunch all day

LUNCH

EL TACORRIDO
drive-thru Mexican taqueria

G'S DYNAMITE DELI
hot and cold sandwiches, pressed
paninis, salads, & soup

HABANERO CAFE
cash-only authentic Mexican
restaurant with breakfast & lunch

POLVO'S
Interior Mexican restaurant famous
for their salsa bar

SANDY'S
burger shack with a walk-up window
& drive-thru

KOKO TIP: 1/4 lb. burger combo for
$4.99 on Thursday + Saturday!

SOUP PEDDLER
order handmade soups, sandwiches,
salads, juices, & smoothies from the
walk-up window

DINNER

ELIZABETH STREET CAFÉ
fancy Vietnamese cafe & French
bakery

KOKO TIP: My go-to order is any of
the spring rolls with the kaffir lime
fried chicken bún.

FRESA'S
one of my favorite restaurants for its
queso, tacos, margaritas, & colorful
patio

LA MEXICANA BAKERY
cheap tacos & fresh Mexican pastries

LENOIR
intimate, romantic restaurant with a
pre-fixed menu & wine garden

SWAY
modern Thai restaurant with an
outdoor dining area

HAPPY HOUR

FRESA'S
Monday to Friday, 3–6pm
$2 off all aguas frescas, botanas, beer, wine, & margaritas

LENOIR
Tuesday to Sunday, 5–6:30pm
in the outdoor wine garden
$5 wine specials by the glass and $3 draft beer

SWAY
Monday to Friday, 3–6pm
at the bar & patio area
half off specialty cocktails, wines, saké, and beer

WINEBELLY
Tuesday to Thursday, 4–6pm
discounted bites and house white, rosé, or red for $5, and local taps for $4

BARS

WINEBELLY
Bohemian wine bar with tapas

DESSERTS

BANANARCHY
frozen bananas dipped in chocolate & assorted toppings

CHURRO CO.
traditional Mexican churro with all the dessert toppings served from a food trailer

DOLCE NEVE GELATO
gelato shop with local flavors & gelato pops

GOURDOUGH'S
big, fat, fried donuts served out of an airstream

LA PÂTISSERIE
bake shop specializing in French sweets like macarons

SUGAR MAMA'S
my go-to for cupcakes in Austin

THAI FRESH
authentic Thai restaurant with home-made vegan ice cream and cooking classes

SHOPS

ART FOR THE PEOPLE
independent gallery showcasing over 120 local artists

BLOOMERS AND FROCKS
vintage women's store specializing in clothing from 1910 through the 1980s

FROND PLANT SHOP
plant shop with houseplants & pots

ESBY APPAREL
women's & men's apparel shop that's designed in Austin

FORTRESS OF INCA
handcrafted & ethically sourced leather shoes from Peru

MANA CULTURE
boho chic clothing & jewelry shop

ROADHOUSE RELICS
art gallery featuring vintage neon art pieces by artist Todd Sanders

PASSPORT VINTAGE
vintage jeans & t-shirts

NOAH MARION

UCHI

ESPRESSO + LEATHER

BEST OF:
SOUTH
LAMAR

TLC

LORO

COFFEE

CAFFÉ MEDICI
lattes, cappuccinos, and cold brew coffee at Lamar Union

MERIT COFFEE
housed inside the Dawson Stone House, a historic landmark building

PATIKA
friendly coffee shop with breakfast, lunch, & brunch

BREAKFAST

MARIA'S TACO XPRESS
Mexican joint known for its tacos & live music

KERBEY LANE
one of the many locations for this 24/7 diner

PICNIK
Picnik's original trailer location that serves grab & go breakfast, lunch, bone broth, & butter coffee

LUNCH

CHI'LANTRO
Korean-Mexican fusion tacos, bowls, and kimchi fries

RAMEN TATSU-YA
second location for the popular ramen restaurant

ODD DUCK
farm-to-table restaurant with seasonally changing New American-style small plates

LORO
Asian smokehouse by James Beard Award winners, Chef Tyson Cole of Uchi and Aaron Franklin of Franklin Barbecue

SANDY'S
burger shack with a walk-up window & drive-thru serving old fashioned hamburgers, hot dogs, and sundaes

SOUP PEDDLER
homemade soups, grilled cheese sandwiches, juices, & smoothies

WHOLLY COW BURGERS
grass fed burgers, cheesesteaks, ruebens, & hand cut fries

DINNER

EBERLY
fancy contemporary American restaurant with a study, patio, & bar

GOURDOUGH'S PUBLIC HOUSE
donut burgers, need I say more?

MATT'S EL RANCHO
fajitas, burritos, flautas, enchiladas, & margaritas

TLC AUSTIN
seafood restaurant with oysters, boiled Texas gulf shrimp, Alaska king crab, and snow crab with 30 beers on tap, cocktails, and wines

SOTO
I really like this Japanese restaurant for its fire salmon

UCHI
if you're looking to splurge, go to Uchi for a contemporary Japanese dining experience

HAPPY HOUR

AVIARY
every day, 4-6pm
$5 bar bites, $2 off all glasses, $2 off all bottled and canned beer, & $10 off select bottles
Saturday, 4-6pm
half off all bottles

BARLATA
Monday, all day
Tuesday & Sunday, after 7pm
half off wine bottles

PINTHOUSE PIZZA
every day, 5-6pm
$2 off pints of Pinthouse beer

LORO
Monday to Friday, 2-5pm
exclusive menu items, $4 boozy slushees, 1/2 off select beer, wine, & sake on tap

UCHI
every day, 5-6:30pm
$3 - $7 drinks, and $3 - $10 bites

BARS

AVIARY
wine bar with Mediterranean influences

THE HIGHBALL
colorful cocktail bar at the Alamo Drafthouse—nightly karaoke, adult comedy, & salsa dancing

BREWERIES

THE ABGB
laid-back brewery that has pizza & sandwiches

DESSERTS

HAYLEYCAKES & COOKIES
custom cookies, cupcakes, & cakes

LICK HONEST ICE CREAMS
creative, artisanal ice cream made with all-natural & local ingredients

NADAMOO! SCOOP SHOP
vegan, coconut milk ice cream shop

THOROUGHBREAD
small-batch bakery that makes really good stuffed cookies

TINY PIES
tiny pies baked in small batches

SHOPS

DYLAN WYLDE
trendy women's clothing shop

KIKI NASS
women's clothing store

NOAH MARION
leather goods store that also makes a fine cup of espresso

NANNIE INEZ
curated collection of home decor & design objects

MOSS DESIGNER CONSIGNMENT
designer consignment store that carries second hand high-end clothing, shoes, & accessories

RADIO COFFEE & BEER

RADIO
COFFEE ⚡ BEER
COCKTAILS
LIVE MUSIC

PIEOUS

BEST OF:
SOUTH
AUSTIN

SOURSOP

ST. ELMO BREWING

COFFEE

BOUGIE'S DONUTS & COFFEE
gourmet donut shop with full-service coffee bar

RADIO COFFEE AND BEER
big coffee shop & beer garden with indoor & outdoor seating

SPOKESMAN
artsy coffee shop located at The Yard

STOUTHAUS COFFEE
coffee, craft beers, pastries, & light bites

BREAKFAST

HIDEAWAY KITCHEN & BAR
southern comfort food restaurant with a Texas twist

KOKO TIP: The griddle cakes are really good.

LUNCH

AVIATOR PIZZA
hand-tossed pizza & Texas craft beer

DEE DEE
northern Thai food trailer with a spicy kick

LIL'DODDY
burger focused restaurant from Hopdoddy Burger Bar group

TACO RANCH
local taco chain with only all-natural ingredients

KOKO TIP: You can get margaritas to go through the drive-thru.

SOURSOP
Pan-Asian food trailer parked at St. Elmo Brewing Company

VALENTINA'S TEX MEX BBQ
Texas barbecue meets Tex-Mex at this food trailer that's worth the drive

KOKO TIP: Order the queso to snack on while you wait.

DINNER

888 PAN ASIAN
Thai, Chinese, and Vietnamese comfort food

KOKO TIP: I like the rice noodle soup with roasted duck and the beef rice noodle.

CANE RUSSO
Neapolitan-style pizzas, salads, desserts, and drinks

DONG NAI
hole-in-the-wall Vietnamese & Chinese restaurant

JACK ALLEN'S KITCHEN
Southwestern comfort food with ingredients from local farms

KOKO TIP: If you like chicken fried steak, try the chicken fried beef ribs.

PIEOUS
really good wood-fired Neapolitan pizza & pastrami

KOKO TIP: The chocolate chip cookies are huge (big-as-your-face).

SAP'S
Thai curries, noodles, & rice plates

SALT TRADERS COASTAL COOKING
fresh oysters, seafood towers, peel & eat shrimp, chowder fries, fish tacos, cocktails, wine, & beer

HAPPY HOUR

CHUY'S
Monday to Friday, 4-7pm

free fully-loaded nacho car, $5 house ritas, $7.95 grande house ritas, $8.99 house Texas martinis, $3.25 domestic beers, $1 off glasses of wine, and $3 off bottles of wine

JACK ALLEN'S KITCHEN
Monday to Friday, 3-7pm

half off appetizers plus drink specials

RED'S PORCH
Monday to Sunday, 3-7pm

$5 appetizers, $5 cocktails, well drinks, drafts, and margaritas

Sunday, all day

$3 mimosas, $6 half-liter mimosas, and $4.75 Bloody Marys

SALT TRADER'S
Monday, 3:30-10pm
Tuesday to Friday, 3:30-6:30pm

drink specials, $1 Gulf oysters, and $5 off beginnings (appetizers)

TRUDY'S
Monday to Friday, 2-7pm

$7 house Mexican martinis, $8 Star of Texas Mexican martinis, $4 house ritas, $3 draft beer, $2 bottle beer, and $5 Deep Eddy flight

BREWERIES

HI SIGN BREWING
veteran-owned independent craft brewery with a taproom & outdoor beer garden

INDEPENDENCE BREWING CO.
craft brewery that has an industrial tasting room

ST. ELMO BREWING CO.
rotating craft taps & an Asian food trailer parked outside at this brewery

STILL AUSTIN WHISKEY CO.
grain-to-glass whiskey distillery & tasting room

THE AUSTIN WINERY
first urban winery producing wine from grape-to-glass in Austin

DESSERTS

AMY'S ICE CREAM
another location for this popular local ice cream chain

COW TIPPING CREAMERY
artisanal soft serve ice cream shop with sundaes, shakes, & floats

KOKO TIP: My favorites are vanilla soft serve in a bubble waffle cone with dark chocolate sauce or the NOLA stacker.

SHOP

THOM'S MARKET
local grocery store with breakfast tacos, coffee, wine, and Texas beers

UNCOMMON OBJECTS
quirky antique shop of eclectic and unique items

119

WEEKEND
GUIDE
TO AUSTIN

AERIAL VIEW OF BARTON SPRINGS POOL

DAY ONE

MORNING

First stop: migas breakfast tacos at Veracruz All-Natural. If you're really hungry, go to Juan in a Million for the legendary Don Juan.

Next, grab a coffee at Cenote and go take a picture at the You're My Butter Half mural.

AFTERNOON

Get in line for barbecue at La Barbecue.

KOKO TIP: Grab a beer from Quickie Pickie before you get in line! If the wait is too long, Micklethwait Craft Meats or Kerlin BBQ are solid barbecue spots, too.

Pack sunscreen and water and go paddle boarding on Lady Bird Lake or swimming at Barton Springs Pool.

NIGHT

Saké social hour at Uchiko.

KOKO TIP: Happy hour starts at 5pm and ends at 6:30pm.

Cocktails at the secret bar, Garage. *Fun fact:* this is Drake's favorite bar in Austin.

Bar hop on Rainey Street–Half Step, Clive Bar, Lustre Pearl, Container Bar, and Bungalow are popular spots.

Late night doughnuts at Gourdough's food trailer on South 1st or a burger at Casino El Camino on 6th.

DAY TWO

MORNING

Start the day with breakfast at Magnolia Cafe. If there's a wait, put your name down and shop next door at Prima Dora and go take a picture around the corner at the Love From Austin mural.

Stop by Jo's Coffee for an iced turbo, then take a picture at the I Love You So Much mural located around the corner!

Explore the shops and boutiques on South Congress.

AFTERNOON

Enjoy tacos, queso, and frozen margaritas on the patio at Fresa's.

Go to Dolce Neve afterwards for handmade gelato.

Take a picture at the Greetings From Austin mural across the street.

NIGHT

Learn how to two-step at the Broken Spoke.

If you're hungry, check out Japanese izakaya at Kemuri Tatsu-ya.

Finish up the night in East Austin with drinks at Whisler's.

KOKO TIP: Pop upstairs to the hidden mezcal bar.

LOVE FROM AUSTIN MURAL AT PRIMA DORA

I LOVE YOU SO MUCH
Musician Amy Cook
Jo's Coffee, 1300 S. Congress Ave.

GREETINGS FROM AUSTIN
Artist Rory Skagen + Bill Brakhage
1702 S. 1st Street

YOU'RE MY BUTTER HALF
Creative Suitcase
2000 E. MLK Jr. Blvd.

LITTLE LIMBO
Designed by Grace Millar &
painted by J Muzacz
1700 S. Congress Ave.

MURALS

SOUTH CONGRESS MURAL
Artist Rory Skagen
1800 S. Congress Ave.

LOVE FROM AUSTIN
Artist Charlie Copp
Prima Dora, 1912 S. Congress Ave.

HISTORIC 6TH STREET
Sanctuary Printshop
Intersection of 6th Street & I-35

TAU CETI
Artist Josef Kristofoletti
Intersection of 2nd St. & Brazos St.

AUSTIN
BUCKET LIST

AERIAL VIEW OF LADY BIRD LAKE

1. **Bat watch from South Congress Bridge**
   (1.5 million Mexican free-tailed bats)

2. **Shop on South Congress**

3. **Try on boots at Allen's Boots**

4. **Attempt Trudy's Mexican martini challenge**

5. **Ghost hunt at The Driskill Hotel**

6. **Play Chicken Sh*t Bingo at Little Longhorn Saloon**

7. **Watch a movie from the private balcony seating at Alamo Ritz**

8. **Play Putt-Putt golf at Peter Pan Mini-Golf**
   (it's BYOB!)

9. **Attempt The Don Juan Taco Challenge at Juan In A Million**

10. **Snap a photo in front of the I Love You So Much mural on South Congress**

11. **Hangover breakfast at Magnolia Cafe**

12. **Wait in line for barbecue at Franklin Barbecue**

13. **Take a picture at the Greetings From Austin mural**

14. **Play with dogs at Zilker Park**

15. **Run the full loop around Lady Bird Lake**

16. **Picnic at Laguna Gloria**

17. **Tour the Texas Capitol**

- 18. Hike the Greenbelt
- 19. Zipline over Lake Travis
- 20. See the sunset from Mount Bonnell
- 21. Smell the flowers at Ladybird Johnson Wildflower Center
- 22. Camp in Emma Long Metropolitan Park
- 23. Take a picture at the You're My Butter Half mural
- 24. Hike to the 360 Bridge Overlook
- 25. Swim at Hamilton Pool
  (reservations required)
- 26. Jump into Barton Springs Pool
- 27. Two-step dance at Broken Spoke
- 28. Hike McKinney Falls
- 29. Dive into Deep Eddy Pool
- 30. Watch an outdoor movie at Blue Starlite Drive-In
- 31. Experience art at Laguna Gloria
- 32. Omakase dinner at Uchi
- 33. Pick fruit at Sweet Berry Farm
- 34. SUP on Lady Bird Lake
- 35. Skinny dip at Hippie Hollow

BUCKET LIST

Share your experiences with me!
@ATASTEOFKOKO #KOKOSGUIDETOAUSTIN

36. Hike Enchanted Rock

37. Dance the night away at Barbarella's

38. Rock out to live music at Mohawk

39. Rope swing into the water at Krause Springs

40. Go on a tower tour of the UT Tower

41. Watch a show at the Historic Scoot Inn

42. Eat a Texas-sized donut at Round Rock Donuts

43. Listen to jazz music at Elephant Room

44. Attend Austin City Limits (ACL) (Sept/Oct)

45. Explore Zilker Botanical Garden

46. Watch a comedy show at Capitol City Comedy Club

47. Volunteer at JBG farms and pick produce

48. Experience the Ellsworth Kelly's Austin

49. Go to a Texas Longhorn football game (fall)

50. Plant shopping at East Austin Succulents

51. Experience Halloween on Dirty Sixth (October)

52. Watch a movie in the park by Austin Parks Foundation

53. Hang out at Blues on the Green (summer)

54. Watch a classic movie & enjoy music at **Sound & Cinema** (summer)

55. Hot fresh donuts from **Mrs. Johnson's Bakery** when the hot sign is on

56. Watch a Broadway show at **Bass Concert Hall**

57. Take bluebonnet photos at **Muleshoe Bend** (April)

58. Experience live theatre performance at **ZACH Theatre**

59. Watch a comedy or magic show at **Esther's Follies**

60. SUP on Lady Bird Lake after dark on an LED-lit paddleboard

61. Ride the **Zilker Zephyr** Miniature Train

62. See the city with **Austin Duck Adventures**

63. Watch a classic movie at **Paramount Theatre**

64. Attend adult night at **Thinkery**

65. Visit the **Austin Central Library** (don't miss the rooftop!)

66. Watch the sunset from **The Oasis restaurant**

67. Watch **JAWS ON THE WATER** by Alamo Drafthouse (summer)

68. Do the **East Austin Studio Tour (EAST)** (fall)

Share your experiences with me!
@ATASTEOFKOKO #KOKOSGUIDETOAUSTIN

Weekend ROAD TRIPS
FROM ↳ AUSTIN

FREDRICKSBERG

DRIPPING SPRINGS

WIMBERLY

SAN ANTONIO

SAN MAR

DRIPPING SPRINGS

DRIVING DISTANCE: 25 miles west

POINTS OF INTEREST:

- Deep Eddy Vodka Distillery
- Desert Door Distillery
- Hamilton Pool Preserve
- Jester King Brewery
- Pedernales Falls State Park
- Treaty Oak Distilling
- The Salt Lick

FREDRICKSBURG

DRIVING DISTANCE: 80 miles west

POINTS OF INTEREST:

- Enchanted Rock
- LBJ National Historical Park
- Fredericksburg Wine Road 290
- Pick-your-own-peach farms

LOCKHART

DRIVING DISTANCE: 30 miles south

POINTS OF INTEREST:

- Black's Barbecue
- Kreuz Market
- Lockhart Chishole Trail Bar-B-Q
- Smitty's Market

ROUND TOP

DRIVING DISTANCE: 80 miles east

POINTS OF INTEREST:

- Junk Gypsy World HQ
- Round Top Antiques Show (Jan, March, & Sept)
- Round Top Vintage Market
- Royers Pie Haven

SAN ANTONIO

DRIVING DISTANCE: 80 miles south

POINTS OF INTEREST:

- The Alamo
- Riverwalk
- The Pearl
- San Antonio Botanical Gardens
- San Antonio Missions

SAN MARCOS

DRIVING DISTANCE: 32 miles south

POINTS OF INTEREST:

- San Marcos River
- San Marcos Premium Outlets
- Tanger Outlets

WACO

DRIVING DISTANCE: 102 miles north

POINTS OF INTEREST:

- Magnolia Market
- Dr. Pepper Museum

WIMBERLEY

DRIVING DISTANCE: 37 miles southwest

POINTS OF INTEREST:

- Bella Vista Ranch
- Jacob's Well

EVENT
CALENDAR

ALLEN'S BOOTS

JANUARY – FEBRUARY

- Austin Oyster Festival
- Austin Marathon & Half Marathon

MARCH

- Rodeo Austin
- South by Southwest (SXSW)
- ABC Kite Festival
- Austin Urban Music Festival

APRIL

- Austin Food + Wine Festival
- Live Fire
- Art City Austin
- Austin Reggae Fest
- Balloons Over Horseshoe Bay Resort
- Eeyore's Annual Birthday Party
- MotoGP™ Grand Prix of the Americas

MAY

- Pecan Street Festival
- Hot Luck Festival
- Austin Fashion Week
- Euphoria Fest

JUNE

- Blues on the Green

JULY

- Willie Nelson's 4th of July Picnic
- H-E-B Austin Symphony July 4th Concert & Fireworks
- Zilker Summer Musical
- Quesoff

- Blues on the Green
- Austin Symphony Hartman Foundation's "Concerts in the Park"

AUGUST

- Austin Chronicle Hot Sauce Festival
- Bat Fest

SEPTEMBER

- Austin Museum Day
- Official Drink of Austin
- Texas Craft Brewers Festival
- Oktoberfest

OCTOBER

- Austin City Limits Music Festival (ACL)
- Texas Monthly BBQ Fest
- Formula 1 United States Grand Prix
- Texas Book Festival

NOVEMBER

- East Austin Studio Tour
- Chuy's Christmas Parade
- Blue Genie Art Bazaar
- Wine and Swine

DECEMBER

- Trail of Lights
- 37th Street Christmas Lights
- Holiday Lights at Mozart's Coffee Roasters
- Armadillo Christmas Bazaar
- Luminations at the Wildflower Center
- Winter Wonderland at The Circuit

NOTES

ELLSWORTH KELLY'S AUSTIN